From Survival
to Celebration

FROM
SURVIVAL
TO
CELEBRATION

Leadership
for the Confident Church

Howard Hanchey

COWLEY PUBLICATIONS
Cambridge ✦ Boston
Massachusetts

Published in the United States of America by Cowley Publications, a division of the Society of St. John the Evangelist. No portion of this book may be reproduced, stored in or introduced into a retrieval system, or transmitted, in any form or by any means—including photocopying—without the prior written permission of Cowley Publications, except in the case of brief quotations embodied in critical articles and reviews.

Library of Congress Cataloging-in-Publication Data:
Hanchey, Howard.
From survival to celebration: leadership for the confident church / Howard Hanchey.
p.   cm.
Includes bibliographical references.
ISBN 1-56101-100-2 (alk. paper)
1. Church renewal. 2. Christian leadership. I. Title.
BV600.2.H29   1994   94-26928
262'.1—dc20   CIP

Cover design by Vicki Black. The manuscript was edited by Cynthia Shattuck and typeset by Vicki Black. The illustrations were developed for publication by Neil Hanchey.

This book is printed on recycled, acid-free paper and was produced in the United States of America.

Additional copies of this book may be purchased from Cowley Publications, 1-800-225-1534.

Second Printing

Cowley Publications
28 Temple Place
Boston, Massachusetts 02111

To
The Department of Pastoral Care
St. Luke's Episcopal Hospital
Texas Medical Center, Houston, Texas

At the invitation of Chaplain Ted Smith, Director of Clinical Pastoral Education, I was privileged to spend the summer of 1993 working as a Chaplain Supervisor with the members of this wonderful department in one of the finest hospitals in the world. I was encouraged by them in the writing of this book, and to these fine folk and the rich faith perspectives they bring to the pastoral care of God's people I offer grateful thanks:

Lucy Arrington (Southern Baptist), Mary Jaquysh (Unity Church of Christianity), Jim Alcorn (Chief of Chaplains, Episcopal), Helen Appelberg (Episcopal), Paul Bennett (Chaplain Supervisor, Presbyterian), Frank Hawkins (Episcopal), Chuck Lightle (American Baptist), Dick Maddox (Disciples of Christ), Milton Odom (Disciples of Christ), Betty Phifer (Missionary Baptist), Rod Pierce (Episcopal), Sue Scott (Southern Baptist), Desmond Thornton (United Methodist), Jim Van Bibber (Southern Baptist) and Jim Wells (Lutheran).

They are among the good and faithful servants to whom Jesus said, "Well done."

CONTENTS

Acknowledgments

T he ideas in this book were tested by clergy and lay leaders from the Episcopal dioceses of Utah and West Virginia and the dioceses of Brandon and Huron in the Anglican Church of Canada; the 1992 Small Church Leadership Conference sponsored by Province V of the Episcopal Church and the 1993 Annual Conference for Small Churches sponsored by Province III; and by students in my classroom at the Episcopal Theological Seminary in Virginia, where I serve as the Arthur Lee Kinsolving Professor of Pastoral Theology. I am grateful to these and many other Christians from several denominations who shared with me their hopes for the church, what they are missing, and what they yearn to hear from leadership. I learned from them all.

I also wish to thank Cynthia Shattuck and Vicki Black, editors at Cowley who helped me focus this work and offered encouragement all along the way. The Studio in Richmond, Virginia, offered wonderful assistance with the illustrations. To all these I also offer grateful thanks.

INTRODUCTION

s I have traveled widely in the church in recent years, more than a few weekend conferences have found me by the fireplace or under a tree talking with Christians from all walks of life. While some were overjoyed with the contemporary Christian church, others expressed disappointment. I began to ask a lot of questions and to catalog the differences. And I found some answers that might surprise you.

Like many in the church, I have been concerned about our loss of spirit and enthusiasm in the last several years. Leaders "challenge" their congregations and end up disappointed by the lack of response. Things that once worked to mobilize the church seem to work no longer. In many congregations enthusiasm is at a low ebb. Still others are diminished by folks who have simply dropped out, disappointed. Many mainline congregations, dioceses, and judicatories today are running out of money. Their leaders are concerned, and sometimes puzzled about why. Numbers are also dropping, and small congregations in particular are scared. Still, the American population continues to expand, and the overall economy continues to grow. So what is the trouble?

Some say this decline is due to the fact that the contemporary church is not aggressive enough about such things as extending an invitation to newcomers. Or aggressive enough to retain them when these folks do come. Or aggressive enough in raising money or in planting new congregations. The list goes on and on. In response, church leaders look more closely at "how to's": how to invite new members, how to assimilate new members, how to raise more money, how to do this and how to do that. "How to's" are good, but they will not reverse the slow decline or the diminished spirit in the modern-day mainline church. There is something wrong which is far more fundamental.

The crisis in the American church is a crisis of faith. Although the church in recent years has created an abundance of new programs (what I call "work news"), at the same time the American church has forgotten how to sing the song of God at work in the world—what the church has always identified as "good news." A doxological theology has disappeared. The church and the world, tired of hearing the song of what the church ought to do and should do, of why this program is important and why that program must be funded, and no longer hearing the song of grace at work in the world, increasingly treats the Christian gospel with indifference. In short, theology and its focus on the work of God in the world has been replaced by a celebration of ecclesiology, the work of the church in the world.

> » Many contemporary congregations, even a majority,
> having adopted an identity based more on what they do
> (maintenance) than on whose they are (mission), are now
> suffering the consequences. People are hungry to hear
> more about God, not the work of the church.

The distinction between a maintenance-minded (work-centered) and a mission-minded (celebrative) congregation stands at the center of this book. In the following pages I will show how the spirit of the church in recent years has been seduced by the ways of the world, and the manner in which some congregations are forming anew their common life by taking a page from the life of the New Testament church.

This book is written to help you think through your ministry of leadership in the church, whether you are a member of the clergy or laity. It can be used as a resource to focus discussion in church governance meetings, and for private edification as well. But it will work best for you if it provides a springboard for a reconsideration of the ministry of the contemporary Christian church, your congregation in particular, and your leadership in your congregation.

In the following pages you will discover a way to diagnose what you believe about God and how you conceive the ministry of the church. As a church leader you will find the ways and means to begin the construction of a mission-minded engine in your congregation. You will learn more about this engine, which is a dynamo. And it is not made by us. It is made by God. It forms vision and generates powerful energy.[1]

Effective church leadership demands three things from us: a tested understanding of leadership itself, a knowledge of the church we presume to lead, and the fundamental task of the church in the world. Clarity about the latter is generally missing in traumatized congregations. The dominant leadership models in today's church are drawn primarily from the secular world and are maintenance-centered, focusing on the work of the church: the strong and decisive *captain of industry,* the *administrator,* the *manager,* the *teacher,* the *caregiver.* What's missing is a style of leadership more truly reflective of the good news of the gospel, one I have learned to call the *celebrant.* Each one of these styles is discussed at length in chapter five and illustrated in chapter six.

To those *new to leadership* in the church: If you're faced with opportunities at once a joy and a bit overwhelming, and if you're not quite sure of the terrain you're on, this book will open vistas and paint pictures of new possibilities. As a result, you will feel increasingly confident and energized to take the reigns of leadership.

And to *"old hands":* If you've been involved in the leadership of the church for some time, and if now you're a bit tired of simply voting on issues and reconciling problems, and if you want to be a bit more proactive and creative in addressing the myriad of opportunities with which God is gifting the church each and every day, this book will help you catch a vision of the possibilities.

And if you are a member of the *clergy,* and if you're not quite happy with the way things have been going; if your ministry has reached more of a plateau than you like, or if by now your ministry is marked by more stress than you like; if signs of burnout are beginning to show, or if you hear reports of "involuntary terminations" with a bit more anxiety than you like, the following pages will help you diagnose your dilemma and claim a new vision.

And to *all leaders* in the church, if you use the ideas in this book to evaluate the shape of your ministry and the spirit of the people committed to your charge, and if they help you re-vision the shape of your leadership, then I hope you will find yourself renewed and refreshed.

Finally, this book is intended for all who are tired of things as they are, who want to move from a maintenance mindset to a mission mindset, and who want to learn the skills that will help them lead their church congregation from mere survival to celebration.

Chapter 1

FROM SURVIVAL TO CELEBRATION

To See Visions and Dream Dreams

Highlights A new breeze is blowing in the contemporary American Christian church. New life is sparking here and there in congregations throughout this land, whether in small towns, growing suburbs, or the inner city. Some congregations are moving from an attitude of church survival to one of celebrating God at work in the world. So what does this new life look like? And can its effects be duplicated?

In this chapter we will look at the differences between what I call maintenance-minded and mission-minded congregations. The theology of the latter approach can be described as doxological, a focus on celebrating God at work in the world on the order of St. Paul's doxology, "Glory to God whose power, working in us, can do infinitely more than we can ask or imagine" (Eph. 3:20). The style of leadership described in this book strongly contributes to a celebrating church and generates from a doxological theology.

Maintenance or Mission?

Two different and distinctive ways of thinking about ministry characterize the contemporary American church. What I have learned to call a *mission mindset* breathes life into the church through celebration, while its opposite, a *maintenance mindset,* consumes the life of the church with its focus on survival.

So what is a mission mindset? What is the shape of this engine able to empower a congregation with joy? Simply this. A mission mindset first of all values the ministry of God at work in the world. It is a mindset that rejoices in the everyday work of God in the midst of life.

A maintenance mindset, on the other hand—and I'll wager that it heavily influences your leadership in the church—values the work of the church in the world. This mindset is often concerned with three items:

1) *sustaining the church*
2) *providing "good works" in the world, and*
3) *making sure the church "shapes up."*

Think with me about the first item, *sustaining the church.* Concerned with the survival of the church and its growth, leaders in maintenance-minded congregations spend much of their time worrying about conservation and preservation. "We've got to have a better Every Member Canvass because we need more money." "We need to get more new members to fill out the budget." Members of those congregations often complain about being tired of requests for more money.

There is nothing wrong with maintaining the church. Good stewardship demands it. But when maintaining the church becomes the first order of business of the church, something important is sacrificed, namely, the church's mission. So now this question: how much of your congregation's common life is focused on sustaining the work of the church? The majority? If it is, most likely you are suffering. If not, what is the main focus?

Now to the second item, *providing "good works" in the world.* "Mission" for maintenance-minded leaders is not the celebration of God at work in the world, but announcements about what the church should be doing in the world. There is a subtle but distinctive difference here. If a mission mindset is strong on theology (the work of God in the world), a maintenance mindset is strong on ecclesiology (the work of the church in the world). In confusing theology with ecclesiology, we forget the wonderful work of identifying and celebrating God at work in the world; its place is taken by programs and issues.

Good works are an important part of the faithfulness of the church, but in recent years their importance has supplanted the celebration of God at work in the world. For example, we in the church may hear much about the will of God for us but not much about God at work taking care of the world everyday. It is almost as though God were absent from the world, though still taking an interest in us. This is not an incarnational theology.

>> Whenever the work of the church is the primary consideration, a mission mindset tends to suffer and a maintenance mindset dominates.

Now consider the third element of a maintenance mindset, *"shaping up" the church*. Strong on the importance of good works and scared about failing to sustain the life of the church, maintenance-minded leaders are forceful in telling their people what they

> ought to do
> should do and
> need to do.

They confuse telling the church what it ought to do with offering a vision to the church; they confuse "work news" with "good news."

Much of the recent three decades of decline in church membership is the result of an overbearing maintenance mindset in the contemporary church. The 1990 *Yearbook of American and Canadian Churches* reports that in 1988 there were 101 million church members in the United States.[1] The U.S. Bureau of Census in that same year totalled the population of the United States at 242.8 million,[2] making church members 41.6 percent of the U.S. population. In other words, among the many religions in America, the Christian church can claim a 41.6 percent market share. But almost three decades earlier—in 1960, with 84.7 million U.S. church members out of a population of 180.7 million—church members constituted 46.9 percent of the total population. This represents a decline of 5.3 percent of the population in just twenty-eight years. In other words, in recent years the Christian churches in America have lost market share. In terms of total population we are *shrinking*.

We are shrinking because many contemporary Christians are tired of hearing about the work of the church on Sunday morning. They are tired of an overbearing narcissism springing from the church's focus on the ministry of the church. They are weary of the worldly focus of the church. More than a few are dropping out. In response to their anger, church leaders often react even more aggressively. They think that in the face of a decline of commitment, spirit, and purpose, redemption can be achieved by a still more accurate identification of issues, by the development of more effective programming, or by the exercise of stronger leadership that tells folks more forcefully what they ought to be doing. But such programs do not work for long.

In his classic book *The Structure of Scientific Revolution*, Thomas Kuhn explains that scientific transitions occur when a new perspective or a new idea shows itself. Joel Barker popularized this notion in his video *Discovering the Future: The Business of Paradigms.*[3] Over and over Barker makes the point that when a new way of thinking sparks into life, a paradigm shift occurs—and the world turns upside down.

That is precisely what happens in congregations newly touched by a praising, doxological, mission mindset.

The Genesis of the Maintenance Mindset

When did a maintenance mindset first assert itself in the church? Think with me about the Christian community in the first and second centuries, when God was close and the early church knew it. Jesus had been recently raised from the dead. These early Christians were standing on the edge of creation. Fire was close, and every time they met there were bursts of energy as stories of the resurrection were freshly told.

These early congregations probably met in one another's homes, though some may have hired rooms for their meetings. By about A.D. 100, Christians were regularly meeting in house churches on Sunday, the first day of the week. For awhile rented rooms or the home of a member sufficed. But as numbers grew, these early Christians began to think of more permanent and accommodating surroundings. Business leaders might have fretted about cash flow, especially those who were paying rent for space in which to gather.

At some point someone began to think about the purchase of a more permanent place to worship. One can almost hear this conversation: "Why should we be renting a room? It's a poor use of our funds. Wouldn't it be a better use of cash flow to buy a building? And wouldn't God be even better glorified with a building worthy of his love? Maybe we should think about a building program." So they built a place for worship. And like the upkeep on many modern-day condominiums, for awhile the costs of owning were incidental. Soon, however, the need for repairs began to show. "The roof has a leak," some observed. And soon this note sounded: "Too few of us are doing too much work." A maintenance mindset began to assert itself.

In the early years of the church the care of the faithful began to take another important shape. Wanting the best for their children, and promising to bring their children up in the knowledge and love of the Lord, Christian parents asked if their infant children could be baptized. To help with their promise to bring up their children in the knowledge and love of the Lord, what we now call Sunday school was born—and with it a need for curriculum materials, supplies, and the annual recruitment of church school teachers. The maintenance of ministry began to take the place of the gospel mission.

Present in all human beings is a tendency toward narcissism, and members of the church are no different. We are driven to consider ourselves—what *we* want and what *we* need—first. We tend to put what *we* value and what *we* want to do for the church and for the world first, too. But our needs—as legitimate as they may be—supply us with an excuse to put our interests front and center. Of course, we righteously assert, our plans are the work to which God calls us! But can you see that through this way of thinking *we* become even more fully the subject of the piece?

> » A maintenance mindset is fundamentally dangerous because it gives expression to our tendency toward narcissism. And as our ministry becomes the subject, thoughts about God at work in the world are shunted aside.

A maintenance mindset is pervasive in the church today: just listen to what we hear from the church. Just read the church press. Listen to church leaders. Listen to sermons. Listen to the everyday conversation of Christians in the world. Theology has given way to ecclesiology, a focus on God has been replaced by a focus on ourselves as the church.

Disabled by Maintenance

The following vignettes portray the troubled spirit of many contemporary Christians, and the way in which a maintenance mindset has discouraged their enthusiasm—even if they are not aware of the diagnosis.

Mary, a middle-aged mother of two, remarks with regret that she simply can't give any more time to the church. "They're always asking for more. I know there are a bunch of things to be done, but I don't have any more to give. Surely church is more than this."

Jim, a retired elder in his church, has turned away from his congregation. "I don't have much to give any more. And that's all I hear from the pulpit. Our preacher is always asking us to do more. There's a new program for this and a new program for that. I don't go to church to feel bad. I need something in which to hope."

Do these stories sound familiar? They give vivid expression to the maintenance mindset crippling the contemporary church. If you are concerned about what you see in your congregation, in the following pages you will find the diagnostic tools you need to isolate this illness.

The debilitating power of the maintenance mindset also shows in an article entitled "At the Crossroads" written by the Episcopal Bishop of Colorado for his diocese. Much concerned with a continually shrinking budget, he writes: "The church in general and our diocese in particular is at a crossroads. We tend to spend most of our time figuring out ways to survive on the road we are on."[4]

In many ways the contemporary mainline church, with its obsessive focus on principles and programs, has given up gospel for garbage. It has given up theology for ecclesiology. When a preacher on Sunday morning fills his or her sermon with a list of what the church

should do,
ought to do,
needs to do,
even what God wants it to do
(the "will of God" syndrome),

with nary a word about the wonderful and everyday work of God in the world, what we have is garbage. A maintenance mindset generates a common life looking more often like politics than grace. And Christians in the pew increasingly are fed up.

» The therapy demanded by this church illness is a revisioning of the mission of the church. Nothing less will satisfy.

A maintenance mindset always pushes for recognition. The following story describes a burgeoning maintenance mindset in a rapidly growing—what many might identify as a "successful"—congregation.

The rector of this church laments that too many in his congregation have given up the "Spirit of God" for a "spirit of renewal." He is making a point about the emergence of a maintenance mindset. This Christian congregation has a long history of a lively, celebrative ministry. God is close and they know it. Stories about God at work in the world (the substance of a mission mindset) abound. Now distinguished by large numbers, a mammoth budget, and buildings overflowing with people, many of this congregation's leaders want to continue growth by focusing on the techniques of renewal rather than celebrating the work of the Spirit bringing them to this place. In other words, the work of growth and success (maintenance) is asserting itself against the celebration of God's action that brought them to this place of living waters (mission).

Now think more closely with me about the way in which a maintenance mindset shows in today's church. Consider the following statement from an article in the *Richmond Times Dispatch* called "Clinton Raises Hopes of Ministry Leaders":

> A congregation's only reason for existence is for people to carry out ministry in the world and to help them learn to live out meaningful lives. Congregations are in the business of equipping people for ministry. This ministry is found in everyday living where everyday people are charged with a call to live together and to make a difference.[5]

What do we have here? A congregation's *only* reason for existence is to do ministry? Where does God fit into this picture? In fact, nowhere but nowhere in this brief discussion of the ministry of the Christian church do we see any mention of the wonderful ministry of God at work in the world. And that is precisely what is wrong with it. Maintenance minded in the extreme, it says much about what the church ought to do in the world, the business of the church in the world, but nothing at all is said about God's ministry in the world.

"Well," you say, perhaps thinking that I overdo it, "in that statement there is at least some *implication* of God's presence." In fact, this statement is strong on ecclesiology—it says a lot about the ministry of the church—and it can seem like it's talking about God. But it is severely short on theology; it says next to nothing about God. It is strong on works, but weak on thanksgiving.

» The contemporary Christian church is strong on programs and issues and short on the celebration of God's ministry in the world. We can either celebrate the work of God in the world—truly *good news,* or celebrate the work of the church in the world, truly *work news.* Modern-day Christians tend toward the latter, and it is killing us.

Another story illustrates the disabling effects of the maintenance mindset. I recently visited a minister who has been with his congregation for three years and quiet disappointment is beginning to show.

I was asked by several members of his congregation, with his encouragement, to present some of the materials in my book *Creative Christian Education*. People seemed to feel they had reached a dead end in the church and in the Sunday school, and they were looking for help. The Saturday conference was over, and as I was preparing to leave the minister told me the following (my own thoughts are in parenthesis):

"What you said today will have a positive effect. Everyone certainly walked away with a new sense of what is possible for us." (*I saw this too, but what they were most excited about was not the new programming materials, which they spooned up like ice cream on a hot day, but my focus on the way in which God is always working on our behalf.*)

"And," he continued, *"things need to change here."* (*I agree—they do. But, I also thought, what really needs to change is the focus of your ministry, going further toward celebration and away from trying to charge your folks with enthusiasm by telling them who they should be and what they need to be doing. You're burning out and burning them out, and you don't even know it.*)

"I'm not thinking of leaving yet," he continued, *"but things can't stay the same."* (*Now we had moved from a reference to the mighty work God was doing in our midst only a short while ago, back to his own quiet despair. Burnout always refocuses on hurt—this is a sure sign of burnout. And because of his pain, he could not hear much of what I said. But I thought I would try.*)

"I find myself hoping that maybe today you saw that when God at work in the world is celebrated, the Spirit reawakens in people's lives," I said. *"In a troubling world, I find that*

many Christians long for this kind of celebration. That's what
seems to have excited your people most of all."
  "Oh, I know that's important," he responded. And then he
paused for a thought. "But really, we've just got to generate
more life here. We've been declining for several years. Oh
well, things will take care of themselves," he added as we
shook hands to part.

My clergy colleague gives a vivid illustration of the trauma
a maintenance mindset visits on the church. It is a powerful
paradigm that is destroying leaders and congregations, but
the depression it generates is not easily identified by those
caught in it. Like many leaders in the church, he is as impres-
sively trapped as a bug in a Venus Flytrap. "Too harsh!" you
say? Only time will tell for him and for the church. But already much of the evidence is in. So about his circumstance
I might also make a prophecy: Eventually he will feel a sense
of failure in this present ministry, and he will leave with disappointment. Maybe even a broken heart. And his congregation will remain—with one, or both.

  » A mission mindset always gives way to a maintenance
  mindset unless vigilance is exercised.

I hope by now you see how easily a maintenance mindset
arises, and how disabling its effects can be. In the church it
primarily values accomplishment and performance, just as
the business world does. But when this mindset takes over in
any congregation's common life—and it generally begins
among the leadership—more and more trauma begins to
show. Members of the church will argue about this and that,
about "my way" and "your way," about what ought to be
done and should be done and needs to be done, while the
celebration of the wonderful work of God at work in the
world is missing.

Celebratory Leadership

Like maintenance-minded leaders, mission-minded leaders are also interested in an organization that runs well, and they are alert to beneficial programs and the identification of appropriate issues. But most of all and first of all, these leaders value identifying and celebrating the ministry of God at work in the world, and they enjoy their capacity to speak of God in plain, everyday language. They know who God is, they have come to expect God to be present in the midst of life, and they know that worship takes place every time they say "Thank you" for a happy coincidence, or for the advent of good fortune. They enjoy centering their attention on God's everyday action in the world, and, as the Westminster Catechism states, they know that the chief aim of the church is to love God and enjoy God forever.

Many years ago one now unknown Christian described what he was looking for in the church. His story is much like the story of many: "I would not give a tuppence to hear from the pulpit where my duty lies, but I would walk a long country mile to hear from whence cometh my help." This Christian affirms a different vision in the church. While Mary and Jim, mentioned previously, object to a quality of leadership strong on programs and issues and short on theology, this old-timer longs to hear about God at work in the world.

>> When knowledge of God's presence and ministry is valued as most important in the local congregation, and when the first order of business is that of seeking to *celebrate* God's presence and ministry in the world, all else tends to fall into place.

In the world at large, mission-minded folks might be called "optimistic." Or "joyful." Or "hopeful personalities." But in the Christian community this mindset, if it springs naturally, also springs from something more lovely still.

Undergirding a mission mindset is a robust christology, one that promotes spiritual growth. Now if you don't call yourself a theologian, please don't be put off by the term "christology," at least until I explain it. And if you do value theology, this will tell you much about what I have learned to identify as a mission mindset in the church.

What is christology? Christology is a way of thinking about the importance of Christ in the world and in the church. The kind of christology present in mission-minded congregations is not, however, highly intellectual. It is not what you are likely to find in a class devoted to the study of dogmatic or systematic theology.

The christology of mission-minded congregations is fundamentally rooted in Jesus' description of his own ministry: the blind see, the deaf hear, and the lame walk (Luke 4:16ff., 7:18ff.). Here is the cross writ large in the midst of life, not as a theological proposition but as an expression of God's presence and ministry. The Sovereign of the universe stoops to be present with us in the midst of our everyday lives. "What wondrous Love is this, O my soul?" exults the old hymn.

Mission-minded Christians believe that Jesus shows us the nature of God. In other words, if you want to know who God is, take a look at who Jesus is and what Jesus did while he was once among us in the flesh. Take a look at his life, death, and resurrection, and you will see God. For the work that Jesus did, that work God still does. Hence, for mission-minded Christians, even today the blind see, the deaf hear, and the lame walk. And I don't mean to suggest that these maladies are necessarily of a physical nature. The blind, deaf, and lame are folk like all of us. And God, in his infinite compassion and mercy, tends us today as closely as Jesus tended those who needed his attention.

Here is a story from everyday life.

Madison Avenue is always dreaming up new ways to help us spend our money. And so it was for Sara. She had lived with the same pair of glasses for fifteen years, and although the style was dated they were still serviceable. "But I began to think, 'It's been fifteen years,'" she said. "'So why not?'"

So Sara made an appointment with an ophthalmologist. He examined her eyes, and then introduced the drops to check for glaucoma. Everything seemed routine until, says Sara, "He began to almost dance around the chair. He was really upset, and though I usually keep my cool, my heart beat fast as well."

"Your eye is ready to hemorrhage," he said, "and there's not a minute to lose. You can go to Johns Hopkins, but I have the equipment to carry out the necessary procedure right here." And so he did.

"If I had not gone to see him when I did, I might have lost the sight in my right eye," she said. "And it would have been too late if I had waited just another month."

Now this question. Why did Sara begin to think about changing her glasses? Was it simply vanity, or was it only good luck? Some will call it fortunate, and it was. And still others may think,

Give an infinite number of monkeys
an infinite number of typewriters, and
one of them will come up with King Lear,
one with Holy Scripture,
one with the Bible with one typo,
and on
and on
and on.

Random chance is infinitely random, and because it is we could, like most of the world, drop our discussion at this point. But Christian theology provides thoughtful alternatives to this somewhat bleak perspective.

To the eyes of faith, God's graceful interest plainly shows in this story. Indeed, Sara's conversation with herself is an expression of a much deeper dialogue with a loving God for whom nothing is of greater interest than her welfare. So was it luck or chance, or was it something more? We may not understand it, nor be able to explain events like these. But they happen, and they do not happen apart from the grace-filled interest of God.

And more: God in Christ also reveals the Sovereign as a companion to folks like Sara, and to all of us. The word companion itself combines the Latin *panis,* meaning "bread," with the prefix *com,* meaning "with." A companion is a friend who breaks bread with us, one joining us at mealtime. The Book of Revelation describes the shape of God's companionship this way:

> I am standing at the door, knocking; if you hear my voice and open the door, I will come in to you and eat with you, and you with me. (Rev. 3:20)

We are not alone in the world, and we are never apart from God's keen and watchful sight. Still more, God's Christ makes it clear in his life, death, and resurrection that God is always in conversation with us. No better illustration of this appears than the way in which Jesus used conversation when he worked in the first-century world, a point also asserted when Jesus joined two disappointed disciples as they trudged toward Emmaus after the crucifixion (Luke 24:13ff.).

» Signs of God's daily care clearly show to mission-minded Christians, and they like few things better than talking about it.

The gospel for mission-minded Christians is not a set of rules about what they should do in the world as faithful Christians, but a wonderful story about what God is doing in the world and in the midst of everyday life today. Mission-minded leaders value the development of this capacity in the churches they serve. Maintenance-minded leaders tend to think there are more important things on the agenda. Where do you stand?

Briefly, this is the christology you will find in this book. To note it early on may, I believe, offer you opportunities to engage a different way of conceiving church life and church leadership in today's world. And I suspect that interest marks the reason you have read this far.

Another story:

> *Two people were walking along a crowded sidewalk in a downtown business area. Suddenly one exclaimed: "Listen to the lovely sound of that cricket." But the other could not hear. He asked his companion how he could detect the sound of a cricket amid the din of people and traffic. The first man, who was a zoologist, had trained himself to listen to the voices of nature. But he didn't explain. He simply took a coin out of his pocket and dropped it to the sidewalk, whereupon a dozen people began to look about them. "We hear," the zoologist said, "what we listen for."*[6]

Mission-minded Christians enjoy, more than anything else, the work of listening and looking for signs of God at work in the world. As a result, their common life rings with both a present strength and a future hope.

So now a question for you as a leader in the church: What is the message of the gospel for the world? How can the gospel be effectively presented? What do you listen for? And what do you hear?

Questions
for Discussion

1. Even at this early point, what new vision of leadership and ministry is now beginning to form for you, or to be confirmed in you?

2. To begin the work of valuing God's ministry "close to home," examine your congregation's history from the perspective of God's ministry. What vision did God generate in your forebears? What signs of God's support showed along the way? When times got tough, how did God help out? Take time to value your church's history, for it is a story, even a pearl of great price.

By developing a picture of your beginnings, and the ways in which you and God have in concert responded with love to your local community over the years, the possibilities of falling in love with God afresh are particularly good—even if, in recent years, you have fallen more in love with maintenance.

Chapter 2

LEADERSHIP IN TODAY'S CHURCH

Lifting a More Spiritual Standard

Highlights A maintenance mindset harshly compromises the life of the church. Instead of focusing church vision heavenward, eyes are cast down at what needs to be done and what ought to be done. What God is doing daily in the world and for the world no longer stands front and center in congregational life. Caring about the church is an important work of the church, and so is caring about the world. Both are spiritual concerns. But people being what they are, when we think of ministry we tend to think of ourselves, while thoughts of God are left out. A more spiritual standard deserves to be developed.

The discussion in this chapter provides a place for you to identify and value the trauma present in many contemporary congregations, and to begin to think about taking action in response. Powerful forces are at work when leaders consider moving the common life of the church from maintenance to mission, even, one might say, of breaking our addiction to maintenance.

A Maintenance Mindset
in Church Leaders

You may now be wondering about how to shift your congregation or your vision of leadership from maintenance to mission. "What is involved?" you might be asking, or "What will it take?" It will take work, because a maintenance mindset is a systemic problem.

Consider the following. Family life in recent years has been carefully reconsidered as one comprising a system of persons in relationship. An important idea generated by the systems approach is this: family patterns continue from generation to generation. A dysfunctional family in one generation is likely to be dysfunctional in the next, unless intervention takes place. Because they have embraced the notion that the primary work of the church is doing good works in the world, many contemporary congregations, denominations, and church leaders now struggle with the dysfunctionality caused by this attitude. And it is a habit that is not easy to kick.

Recently, a member of the clergy described to me the emergence of a maintenance mindset in his life, and the way it adversely compromised his ministry. In his recitation, watch as he moves away from an initial celebration of God at work in the world (mission and its celebrative theology) toward a caretaking ministry of the church (maintenance with its focus on ecclesiology), and then, after a number of years, moves back again to a mission mindset.

A genuine excitement marked my life when I began to think about the possibility of ordained ministry. I felt that God was close—not only to me but to the world. My enthusiasm carried for a good while, but then I began to lose it, not recognizing the loss at the time.

For the most part my enthusiasm was harshly compromised by seminary education. In seminary I was overwhelmed by the task of looking at the Bible from academic and critical perspectives: who wrote what and why it was written, the dates of the writing, what was probably Jewish or Christian in origin—and what was not. And there was ever so much more. Courses in theology, ethics, and history made what I thought to be a real theologian and pastor out of me. But in reality this did not happen: what follows did.

Having been taught in the classroom what was "right" about the Bible and what was not, what mature Christians ought to believe and what could be judged heretical, what the church at its best ought to believe and should believe, and what Christians and the contemporary church should do and ought to do in the face of an often times complex and puzzling world, I began to treat my people in a similar fashion. I told them what they ought to do and should do, even what God wanted them to do. I forgot to tell them about what God was doing in the world.

But the story of my "fall from grace" is even more tragic. I had no idea about what I was doing. I wasn't even remotely critical about what I was leaving out. Marshall McLuhan, the communications whiz, describing the power of television as an educational medium, accurately describes what happened to me. The medium of the seminary classroom and the medium of being an excellent student who had it all together strongly suggested this message: at my best I should want to help the church achieve a similar excellence. So—to get right to the point—I was strong on oughts and shoulds, my sermons often sounded like lectures, and questions in a discussion group were not valued by me as an opportunity for others to grow, but for me to give the answers. One could say I was more aware of the law than I was of grace every-day at work in the world. Or, to put it another way, I gave up the gospel message for a message of work.

I told my people, encouraged my people, in every way tried to sell my people on the importance of being a responsible Christian in the world. Over the years my church created

community programs that, in the long run, never quite satis-
fied anyone. Every year I had to plug away at finding teach-
ers for the Sunday school, and encourage my people to be
faithful in their devotions and church attendance. Month af-
ter month and year after year energy was spent. And there
was not much satisfaction for me (or for my people) in re-
sponse. I had become a caretaker of the church and a parent
to my people, and I had lost a vision of God at work in the
world. I began to realize something was missing.

Then—some could say by accident but I can only say by
grace—on the occasion of a complex program falling ser-
endipitously into place, a friend remarked that God had been
good. "God was good," I thought, almost dismissing it. But
then I heard it: "God is good." And there, in that moment and
in that place, a journey that had been for the most part put
on hold for several decades began afresh. From that moment
I began to value afresh the work of God in the world. I also
discovered that other clergy were doing the same thing. And I
also heard in the stories of caretaking clergy the same tired
resonances that once characterized my ministry.

I'm not saying that I have all the answers. But your descrip-
tion of moving from maintenance-minded to mission-minded
leadership is an elaboration of my journey, and it also cele-
brates in large measure the way I see things now.

» What signs of mission and maintenance show in the
narrative of this man's story? What are the points of connection with your journey?

Here's another perspective. During the summer of 1993,
Pope John Paul II made a long anticipated trip to the United
States on the occasion of a world youth day rally. Some
called this event a modern-day Roman Catholic Woodstock.
And so it proved to be.

More than 350,000 young people visited Denver, Colorado
for this weekend event. The Bishop of Rome used this occa-

sion to call close attention to the moral dilemmas faced by many in today's world (the overuse of drugs, abortion, promiscuity) as well as in the church (whether priests should be married or celibate, whether women should be ordained). In summary, he warned those at the Sunday mass, "You should not be ashamed of the gospel. You should be proud of the gospel."

The Pope's Sunday message was full of oughts and shoulds, what these young Christians

> *need to do,*
> *ought to do, and*
> *should do.*

It was a message strongly focused on obligation and responsibility, truly maintenance minded. Admittedly, the issues about which Pope John Paul II spoke are important. But he, like many leaders in the church, also missed an important point. There is a *big* difference between telling folks to be proud of the gospel and sharing with the world the gospel of what God is doing in our midst.

Instead of calling his hearers to think about themselves, focusing on who *they* are and where *they* needed to go—which is the maintenance mindset in a nutshell—Pope John Paul II could have chosen to celebrate the wonderful work of God bringing together in one great and mighty act of worship some 350,000 expectant and hopeful young people. He could have delighted the world with news of a living God providing food and lodging and care—the logistics are staggering—for all these folk. Granted, everything was not perfect, as if it can ever be in a broken world. But even admitting what went wrong, this event was a magnificent testimony to One whose spirit blows through the world, moving the world to a response of love and care. Indeed, in the moment of the Denver event, God multiplied loaves and fishes. Here is truly living gospel, not the *memory* of a gospel of which the church still ought to be proud.

"But," some of you may say, "there is not one bit of proof that God had anything to do with this!" And there is, of course, no proof. But that doesn't prevent a mission mindset from seeing afresh that God is doing in the world today what Scripture shows God once did in the world. It is a matter of faith, isn't it? And because it is a matter of faith, mission-minded Christians have learned to be celebrants of God at work in the world. After all, how else will the world know who cares about us so much?

> » Can you distinguish between a focus on the church—
> what the church ought to do and should do—and a focus
> on God—what God is doing in the world? Which would
> you rather hear about? Which do you think the church
> would rather hear about? Which do you think the world
> would rather hear about?

A maintenance mindset is helpful and useful in the church. But when maintenance comes first, the celebration of the work of God in the world takes second place. Both are necessary, but only when mission comes first does the life of the church sing with joy.

While attending a conference in a midwestern state, one participant latched onto my notion of the gospel as "singing the song of angels." Here's her story.

I came into the church because I heard the song of angels. God was close and I knew it. I was touched by grace and all my life was changed.

Becoming active in the church, I was later elected to several leadership positions. From the beginning my enthusiasm never waned, but for some reason the joy of those early years never returned. I thought that maybe my spiritual journey could be likened to a honeymoon; no honeymoon can be expected to last.

As a church leader I wanted others to know what I knew. And I also wanted to be responsible to a church I loved. My ministry was strong on organization and calling the church to responsibility, so the song I sang was a song of oughts and shoulds. But no matter how much I sang it, the joy I had once was never revealed again. I lost the way. Now I see what I did wrong. I gave up the song of angels for the song of work.

I still hear from this Christian woman, and every time I do, with it comes also a word of thanks for a perspective that helped her recast her faith. Organization is important in the life of the church, and so is taking care of the church and the world. But when organization and caretaking walk first in the life of the church, the song of angels dims, and good news is replaced with work news. The faith of the church is at issue here, and what we have in the church is a crisis of faith.

Work News Versus Good News

The story is told of the faithful Lutheran who, on the occasion of her death, found herself at the gates of heaven in conversation with St. Peter. Having lived a righteous life and being justified by grace through faith, she was extremely put out when Peter told her she did not have the credentials for entrance into heaven. Pointing to a side road leading down the hill to perdition, he was adamant. Resigned, she left. Upon reaching that place of absence and horror, in the corner she saw a recognizable figure. "Martin!" she cried. "Martin! Martin! What are *you* doing here?" "I was wrong," he said. "Oh, was I ever wrong! It wasn't grace—it was works all along!"[1]

Of course it was not works, and of course it is grace: but the story makes its point.

Work news in the church is rooted in large measure in theological deism. Deism asserts that God is out there in the heavens somewhere, and the church is left in the world to do God's work in the world. This kind of teaching is strong on rules and regulations about what the church should do to honor God's more-or-less absent ministry. Many articles in the church and denominational press offer a not surprising illustration of the deism of the maintenance mindset.

Choose a denominational newspaper near at hand. Now read from the first page. I suspect you will find that both local and religious news stories are far more focused on the work of the church in the world than on celebrating the everyday miracles of God in the world. And even if the good works of the church are offered to the glory of God, which of course they are, these "programs of love" are mostly described as the *ministry of the church*. A maintenance mindset rules.

The front page of the November 1993 issue of *Episcopal Life* (the national publication of the Episcopal Church) offers a good illustration. Its headlines announced:

DIOCESES SOUND ALARM TO NATIONAL STAFF
BROWNING FINDS LOVE, ANXIETY ON MEXICAN TRIP
HISTORIC PARISH IN CANAL ZONE STRUGGLES
WITH CULTURAL CHANGES

In none of the stories following these headlines is there any mention of God at work in the world.

"But," you say, "such stories might appear on an inside page." Not so. In fact, page three represents the rest of this periodical:

Connecticut Bishop Chosen for Europe
Chinnis Taps Priest As No. 2 Deputy
Illinois Priest Elected in Ohio
West Texas Elects Bishop Coadjutor
Bishop in Quincy to Join "Splinter"
Costa Rican Churches Team Up Against AIDS
Ministry Office Gets Coordinator
Public Health Expert Heads AIDS Coalition
Majority of Dioceses OK Jelinek as Bishop

Again, on this page there is no mention of God's mighty acts in today's world, and the daily miracles God is everyday working in our behalf.

"Well," you say, "you trivialize God. God doesn't have time for folks like me." So take that up with Scripture's witness. No wonder that many in the world figure the church and the gospel are both anachronisms. There *is* important news to be shared within the community of faith about operating the community of faith. But news about "us" has far surpassed news about God: in the pulpit on Sunday morning, in Christian education, and in the books and periodicals we publish. News about "us," stories about what faithful Christians ought to do—work news—has supplanted the good news about God at work in the world.

Local church newsletters fare no better. A headline in a church bulletin asserts, "Have You Heard the Good News?"— the "good news" being a garage sale sponsored by a church stewardship committee. If you believe this story is an aberration, read your own newsletters. Still another headline in a local bulletin reads, "Volunteers Needed" followed by a plea for help with the Sunday school. A maintenance mindset clearly shows. Now again this point: a concern for maintenance is necessary in the church, but when it sounds in the majority, which it generally does today, the church invariably becomes depressed.

"But," you say, "could these church newsletter stories express a mission-mindset?" Yes, they could, and here's how.

First, look with me at the article about the *garage sale.* Using about the same amount of space, this article could have developed the notion that God at work in the world is, by inspiring garage sales, helping the children of the world recycle used materials—often at a better value than when new. If the article had taken this tact, a wonderful note of Christian stewardship could have also sounded. As a result, the reader might have come away with the idea that "God is good" rather than "I should go to that garage sale." To reframe the article in this fashion, the writer would have needed only to make *God* the subject of the story, not *attendance* at the sale. To do this would also require the author to take a leap of faith, to identify God at work in the world in these events.

Second, the article on *volunteers for the Sunday school* could have developed the idea that right at this moment God is making new this year's Sunday school, and "your participation is not to be missed because it will change your life for the good." "Wild!" you say. "Could teaching in the Sunday school ever be this satisfying and life-giving?"

>> A maintenance mindset refocuses every discussion so that it centers on the ministry of the church, leaving out the celebration of God at work in the world.

Mission or Maintenance:
Still Not Sure?

If you are still unconvinced, perhaps you are asking: "Is a maintenance mindset truly at the root of our problem? Can it be more? Or even something else?" In fact there are several other popular interpretations offering a different view of the contemporary predicament of the church.

First, some see the current trauma in the church as part of a *liberal/conservative conflict,* a diagnosis holding some promise. Liberal Christianity has in some measure given itself wholeheartedly to issues and programs in recent years, assuming that "We are the hands and feet of God in the world." With its focus on issues and programming, what liberal Christianity gives up is the work of identifying and celebrating God at work in the everyday world, a focus I believe has been largely retained by conservative Christianity. About conservative Christians a liberal Christian might say, "They're just fundamentalists." In fact, one might say that liberal Christianity has failed to distinguish between fundamentalism and fundamentals.

Liberal Christianity on the whole often substitutes the necessity of the church doing God's work in the world for the celebration of God at work in the world. In other words, the work of religion has been substituted for the joy of faith. In their book *Toxic Faith* authors Stephen Arterburn and Jack Felton warn, "Toxic faith is a destructive and dangerous relationship with a religion that allows the religion, not the relationship with God, to control a person's life."[2] In fact, when mission gives way to maintenance, a lively faith that sees God at work in the world tends to give way to an interest in religious works. Maintenance subverts mission; it happens in the church year after year.

A recent study also suggests that Christians who believe God is at work in the here and now of everyday life are more optimistic than those Christians who do not. In this study, authors Sethi and Seligman also say that Christians who believe "God is always with you" tend to be more optimistic about life.[3] A mission mindset *does* make a difference.

A second line of interpretation of church trauma holds that the remedy for a shrinking church is *more effective programming.* Even conservative Christians, taking a page from the liberals and hoping to renew congregational life, have come to believe that issue identification and programming will make for church growth. True, carefully constructed church growth programs do often generate bursts of short-term enthusiasm. But without a strong theological underpinning, such enthusiasm generally gives way to long-term despair: "Maybe we had better try something else," or "We've got to get more help" with this or that task, because "I'm burning out."

But more and better programming is a vain hope for long-term renewal in the church; it is like telling a couple in marital trauma to rearrange the living room furniture. Now rearranging the living room may provide a short-term lift for some couples, but such a spirit quickly plays out. The trauma is too deep. And the trauma in much of the contemporary Christian church is too deep for the quick fix of better programming.

Third, many contemporary congregations are benefitting from the *return of baby boomers* and their children, who are called the "baby busters." Faced with growing numbers, many maintenance-minded congregations too quickly assume they are doing things right, when in fact it is not the health of their common life that is attractive, but that these boomers are looking for a place to call home.

Some of the leaders of these same congregations also say that boomers and busters are looking for a church able to deliver "feel good" experiences. If those experiences are not forthcoming, they warn, the boomers will simply "shop" elsewhere. Perhaps they will. But will they stay even in that new place? Can the greed for something new ever be satisfied?

In fact, many of these folks, raised on a steady diet of secularism, are hungry to hear more about God. They are not much interested in the affirmation of creedal principles, nor are they much interested in identifying with one denomination over against another. Having never heard much about God, now they want to hear more. In their emptiness they are not interested in highly intellectualized discussions about church doctrine, liturgical practice, or creedal affirmations: they want to know who God is. Many have been touched by grace and want to know its Source, and they tend to flock to those churches that celebrate the bread of life everyday in the midst of life.

In the long run these baby boomers and baby busters are looking for far more than maintenance. To treat them—or anyone—as persons simply looking for another "feel good" experience is to miss the hunger truly bringing them to church, and to miss God's action in bringing them to places of living waters. Doubtless many *are* looking for effective programming; I certainly do when I go to church, and there is nothing wrong with a hunger for excellence. But these new-comers are also looking for much deeper things. They are looking for a lively faith and a word about God at work in the world, something they missed in their growing-up years. To treat them only to effective programs without providing a more healthful substance is simply to discount their heartfelt hunger. What the church believes about God will keep them. Or it will lose them.

So what of the future? The answer beginning to show itself is this: the congregations that are most vital, alive, and confident today are those who have learned afresh to identify and celebrate the work of God in the world. And because it is told with joy and affection, these modern-day Christians sing a song sounding a lot like the celebration of the first-century church.

Questions
for Discussion

1. What ideas in this chapter illuminate your concept of leadership and ministry? What hope do they provide? As a result, how might you reshape your vision for ministry?

2. What signs of "work news" show in your congregation's common life? Distinguishing between "work news" and "good news" in your ministry will go a long way toward providing a positive model for your people.

3. Where a maintenance mindset is in the majority, it does not give way easily to mission. Parishioners may just not "get the point." Some might say "Talking about God *is* really important, but we've got work to do." Like every human institution, the church tends to stick with old and familiar patterns, even when those patterns abuse all hopes for the future. Where do you anticipate resistance as you think about helping your congregation move from maintenance to mission?

Chapter 3

A THEOLOGY OF CELEBRATION

Divine Glory or Dry Bones?

Highlights How does a mission-minded theology show itself in day-to-day living? Theology makes an important difference in the way leadership is exercised in the contemporary church. If God is viewed as "out there," leadership will often be strong on programming and good works—taking care of God's world.

A mission mindset, on the other hand, believing that God's presence and ministry are as close to the world as the air we breathe, generates leadership of a different kind, as well as a different kind of congregational life. If maintenance-minded congregations are overburdened with work to be done and responsibilities to be shouldered—an attitude causing chronic depression in the people of God—mission-minded communities, because they know God is closely present in the here-and-now of everyday life, burn with an expectant and hopeful spirit.

The following pages paint a picture of the spirit of a mission-centered theology, and do so always in relation to a story from the here-and-now of everyday life. This chapter does not pretend to offer a complete discussion of the theology underlying the life of a mission-minded Christian, but the picture it paints of the joy and optimism generated by this mindset is right on target.

Horizontal and Vertical Theologies

The doxological, celebrative theology present in mission-minded congregations is what some church leaders are now calling a horizontal theology, as opposed to a vertical theology. So what does this mean, and why might the concept of a horizontal theology be important in helping us understand the newness showing itself here and there in the American church?

Across America many nondenominational community churches are growing, many at amazing rates. More than a few of these congregations are also growing where growth should not be taking place and spirits and enthusiasm should not be high, such as in locally depressed economies. Possessing what Brad Hall, an Episcopal priest in Palm Desert, California, and others identify as a horizontal theology, these celebrating congregations employ a theology that values the work of God in the everyday world.

A vertical theology—and most mainline denominations are strong on this—is strongly based on creedal affirmations, such as "I believe in God, the Father Almighty, Maker of heaven and earth...." Such a theology is, to many modern-day people, too abstract. What they hunger for is a note of the personal in theology. They are looking for something in the midst of life about which to give praise and thanksgiving, not an idea to affirm.

What creedal congregations must learn afresh is that doctrine and creed do not easily help people see God at work in the world. Nor do they help people fall in love with God. Stories of God at work in the world and in our lives best accomplish this.

» If a horizontal theology is primarily interested in helping
people fall in love with God, a vertical theology is designed
to help people believe in God. They are not the same thing.

"So," you ask, "how come so many Christians, touched by
God's love and in love with God, begin to push doctrine instead of love?" It is a good question. In fact, having been
touched and welcomed by grace to a relationship with God,
next these Christians try to help their newfound friends—
even the world—believe in what they now know and enjoy.
But belief can never do the work of love. When they meet
with resistance, even a lack of understanding, these Christians tend to explain faith, share doctrine, press for belief,
and find themselves confounded when the world turns away.
Only love warms the heart. Mission-minded congregations
are strong on telling their stories of God's wondrous love, and
the world is more likely to respond with love to a love that
first loves us.

» Creedal congregations suffer because they mistake the
proclamation of doctrine and creeds for good news stories
of God at work in the world.

Too strong of a focus on creeds and doctrine also generates a maintenance mindset. These emphasize what the
church and the world ought to believe about God, as distinguished from the work of celebrating what God is doing in
the world. First things first, one might say: and when doctrine
and creed come first, the church suffers.

What the growth of nondenominational community chapels is showing the mainline churches is this: many in the
world are not hungry for the highly intellectual language of a
creedal affirmation, particularly when what suffers is the
celebration of God at work in the world. These chapels are
calling the mainline churches to account for excessively pro-

moting Christian belief at the expense of celebrating the work of God in the here-and-now of everyday life.

Think about the theology present in your congregation. Is it primarily horizontal or vertical? Certainly elements of each are appropriate, but if a horizontal theology is not present, it is likely that stories about God at work in the world are also absent.

A keen interest in the workings of God lies beneath the vitality of a gospel-converted, mission-minded congregation. Now I don't mean to suggest that the power of God is not present in the most intractable of maintenance-minded congregations, or in their leaders. Nor do I mean to suggest that any person can understand more than a tiny bit about who God is and how God works in the world. But mission-minded congregations have learned this: the celebration of the power of God, as revealed in Scripture, creates joy in their common life, not the necessity of fixing the roof. Strong-willed, maintenance-minded congregations have lost this vision.

One Christian writer put it this way.

> Finding God is not finding a Reality strange and new; it is recognizing and responding to Someone whom we have always known, although perhaps we knew it not. It is answering "Yes" to a Voice one has often heard, but to which heretofore one may not have been willing or prepared to listen. But that Voice, though it speaks in our hearts, is not our voice. It comes from heights and depths we cannot scale or fathom. And the words the Voice speaks are not ours. They are the words of the One who is as far as he is near, in whom alone our partial, thwarted lives have meaning and wholeness, and for whose sake alone even the least of these little ones has infinite worth.[1]

I hope by now this is clear: theology—particularly a horizontal, incarnational theology—helps the lives of mission-minded Christians ring with joy. Theology for these folk is not highly intellectual, philosophical, and abstract. Rather, mission-minded Christians use Bible stories as windows into the ways in which God is present in the world today. As a result, these contemporary Christians say thank you every day for blessings that fill their cup to overflowing.

Now this said, mission-minded Christians are just as subject as the rest of the church to the vicissitudes and harsh realities of everyday life. But they never let bad times turn their eyes from the conviction that in the midst of life there is the presence of Another always doing more than they can ask or imagine.

> » Always the choice is before us—even in the midst of a
> complex and often adversarial world—to see divine glory
> or dry bones. How do you see it?

The Gospel in Practice

It might be said that mission-minded Christians practice the gospel in a way that maintenance-minded Christians do not. So how does one practice the gospel? The answer to this question goes a long way toward offering an understanding of the delight that shows among mission-minded Christians. In large measure these Christians practice the gospel by sharing stories like the following.

One Sunday morning Mike Crawford related to others an event that happened earlier in the week. Traveling to work early one weekday, Mike found himself behind a flatbed construction truck loaded with the heavy forms necessary to shape a building foundation.

"I was not too close to the back of the trailer and making good time, just thinking about the day ahead, when suddenly I thought to myself: that equipment is heavy-duty stuff. What if it should shift on a bump and fall off? Maybe I'd better move." Glancing in his rearview mirror and seeing the way clear, Mike moved into the adjacent lane. And just as he did

so a piece of equipment shifted and fell, cartwheeling into the place he had just been and then to the side of the road.

"I saw it all in my rearview mirror," said Mike. "And I said a prayer of thanks right there."

Now some Christians might say, "What a great story," or "Isn't that nice?" and then move on to more weighty matters like "What is the next order of business?" Still others might say that Mike was simply the beneficiary of good luck or good fortune, on the order of

give an infinite number of monkeys
an infinite number of typewriters
and one of them will,
theoretically,
come up with
this scenario,
this scenario with one amendment,
and the list goes on and on and on.

But the plain fact is this: random chance is made up of an infinite and random number of possibilities, sort of like the lottery. But is life only a lottery? What can be said of God's presence and ministry? Christian theology offers a thoughtful alternative to this somewhat bleak perspective. God is at work in the world, and mission-minded Christians like nothing better than the opportunity to point out signs of the kingdom of heaven at hand. That is always the first order of business in mission-minded congregations.

The illustration on the next page describes several of the key aspects of the mission mindset, including the importance of giving thanks in all things.

THE CELEBRATIVE MISSION MINDSET

1) Mission-minded Christians, knowing the kingdom of heaven is always at hand, and still further knowing that all of life is a gift from God, are blessed with an expectant, hopeful attitude. In short, they are celebrants.

2) Check out the breadth of your mission mindset. What gifts from God do you see in the world around you? In your surrounding community? Your church? In your life? List them below. Compare and contrast them with the "oughts" and "shoulds" suggested in the picture of congregational stress and burnout.

Gifts from God

Vision is lifted heavenward by leadership.

3) The weight of these items is light. In fact, the ability to identify God at work in the world tends to generate energy and enthusiasm in the church. This has been so since the first century.

4) Feeling hopeful and confident, not at all alone in the world, mission-minded Christians are expectant and joyfilled.

The Bottom Line: The life generated by a mission-mindset stands in stark contrast to that generated by a maintenance mindset. Theology makes all the difference. Notice how the items you list above lift one's vision to heavenly things. This yoke is easy and its burden is truly light (Mt.11:30). Such a vision and such an attitude mark the lives of mission-minded Christians with celebration.

Giving Thanks to God in All Things

Many Christians are hesitant to ascribe to God a ministry like the one in Mike's story, mainly because they fear that the response of the world might be something like: "If your God is so good, then why is there so much suffering in the world?"

While not denying that bad things happen in the midst of life, mission-minded Christians are not willing to give up opportunities to praise God for the blessings that accrue in the world every day. As a consequence, these folks have also learned to respond to—and even answer—the world's hard questions from a perspective of human freedom, sin, natural law ("what goes up must come down"), the forces of evil that seek to destroy life, mystery, and miracle. Again this point: theology makes a difference.

Mission-minded Christians also know that no matter how many bad things occur, Jesus asked this poignant question: "Who among you, if a child asks for bread, will give a stone?" These Christians long ago learned that God doesn't function like an abusive parent. And while God may be portrayed that way in some parts of the Bible, in fact these stories say a lot more about their authors than about the breadth of God's love for us.

By now some of you might be thinking that perhaps this mission-minded attitude of thanksgiving is a bit overdone. Not so—and this is why. To understand prayer better and more completely, over the centuries the Christian church has distinguished seven different kinds of prayer, always listed in the following order:

1. Adoration (of God and directed toward God)
2. Praise (to God)
3. Thanksgiving (for gifts from God)
4. Penitence (saying we are sorry)
5. Oblation (offering to God)
6. Intercession (asking God in behalf of others)
7. Petition (asking God in behalf of ourselves).

Notice the three that are first. Mission-minded Christians and their leaders, touched by the love of God, simply enjoy offering to God adoration, praise, and thanksgiving always and everywhere.

> Just as the bright light of a wonderful sunrise naturally brings joy to so many at the beginning of the day, so mission-minded Christians, knowing God's love because they have been taught to identify it in the world, simply cannot help but sing in response.

Maintenance-minded Christians have trouble at this point. They just don't get it—"Now that we've said a prayer, let's get on with business!"

In the Valley of the Shadow of Death: Hope and Suffering

Mission-minded Christians and their leaders believe that "if God be for us, who can be against us?" With some of the theological perspectives previously noted in this book, they are able plainly to see God at work in a sometimes confusing and often complex world. What follows is a far from complete discussion of these issues, but it does paint a picture of the way in which these Christians interpret life from the perspectives of adoration, praise, and thanksgiving.

Mission-minded Christians are empowered in their ministry of identification by strong programs of adult education dealing with issues like suffering and hope. Sermons address these same questions, as do Bible studies and prayer groups. Even the meetings of boards and committees often open with the kind of prayer and biblical reflection that make for theological clarity.

Now return with me to the story of Mike. In offering a spiritual interpretation of a potentially dangerous event, Mike was drawing upon his ability to identify and celebrate the work of

God in the world. And in doing this work, Mike greatly depended upon the ministry of Jesus.

Why did Mike begin to think that danger might be lurking on that truck bed? And why did he begin to think about moving to another lane? Was it simply luck and good fortune—or was there more? Jesus provides a helpful guide. Think with me about this story and its relationship to the christology presented in chapter one: the blind see, the deaf hear, and the lame walk (Luke 7:18ff.).

Mission-minded Christians would suggest that Mike's deaf ears were opened as he heard a voice without sound but with a care-filled interest as broad as the universe. In fact, mission-minded leaders know that when they are gifted with a new idea, or when the solution to a knotty problem shows itself, or when a congregation mobilizes itself to an important task, God is revealed anew as the blind find their sight, the deaf hear afresh, and the lame are strengthened to walk.

"But why," you ask, "doesn't God do this for all of us?" In fact, not a thing happens in life that is not of keen interest to God. But in our conversation with God we simply don't listen fully. And sometimes we are even unable to listen, given the noise of our lives.

> » Mission-minded Christians are quick to acknowledge mystery and to accept their responsibility for what goes wrong in the world. But they are just as quick to declare that God is deeply interested in all of us and that the daily signs of God's care clearly show in the world.

Hence, whenever mission-minded Christians see *vision* where there was formerly none, an *idea* where there was once a question; when a seeming insurmountable problem is *resolved,* a knotty issue *clarified,* a ruptured relationship made *whole;* when there is *movement* where there was once stagnation and *concern* where there was hurt, they are recognizing a sovereign God's ministry in the here-and-now of everyday life. And recognizing it, they often offer words of praise and thanksgiving to one another.

Freedom and God's Faithfulness:
For Thou Art With Me

Freedom sets human beings at liberty to listen first of all to ourselves and what we believe to be our best interests. In our example, Mike was alert to a word of grace on a morning several years ago; on the other hand, he could have been so preoccupied with other cares and worries that he failed to listen or hear this word. There have been countless other times in Mike's life, and in yours and mine, when we (and he) did not or could not or were not able to listen to a Voice of care as wide as the universe. Such is life, but such also is Love.

Consider the following story and think about what it suggests about human freedom and God's care for us.

Many years ago a young girl sold newspapers on a street corner in Louisville. Her family was poor and she had to earn some money to help put food on the table. One Sunday morning, she was selling newspapers on Second Street across from Christ Cathedral when a woman walked across the street to where she was standing. The girl could tell the woman was gentle and kind, so she was not afraid.

The woman said to the girl, "What are you doing here? Why are you selling newspapers?"

When the girl told her that she needed the money to live on, the woman said, "Come with me" and took her by the hand and led her across the street and into the warmth of the cathedral. There she found some food for her to eat and a good heavy coat to wear.

The woman kept up with the child and saw that she came regularly to Sunday school. The girl grew up to be a young woman, and all her life she stayed close to the cathedral and gave thanks for the woman's kindness and the beautiful ca-

thedral congregation.

This story has not ended. The young girl is much older now. She lives which much physical pain most of the time, and she rarely leaves her small apartment. But she still loves the cathedral, and she is still, with thanksgiving, receiving the pastoral care and love of the cathedral's ministry.

"Somehow," continues the story's author, "this true story speaks to me of the history of our lovely cathedral, which down through the many years of her ministry has reached out with her loving arms of Christ and has thus embraced and sheltered God's children."[2]

Why should a young girl find it necessary to sell newspapers to make ends meet? And why would a woman of means choose to address her need?

It doesn't seem fair that a child should encounter poverty so near. Although no mention is made of her family, one might surmise that they were without many worldly goods. Their poverty might have sprung from several causes: an inadequate education, doors of opportunity closed, a crippling family history. And why should any adult who is the parent of such a child struggle every day with putting bread on the table because a full-time job simply does not pay enough? Living from hand-to-mouth is tough on anyone, and when the paper-thin margin for emergencies evaporates, life is particularly tough.

But God cares. So what was God to do for this young girl, a child of his, and her family, all without sufficient means to engage the world? What God did was this: God created an idea, an opportunity, a new possibility, for this child and her family and the woman who reached out to her.

Life, to eyes of faith stirred by the Bible's witness, is as full of miracles today as it has ever been. Free we might be, but by God's grace we are loved also.

» All is not fair in the world. But mission-minded Christians know that always the world belongs to God, and that signs of God's care every day show even in the midst of chronic pain and suffering.

The Kingdom of Heaven is Like...

In still another way the story of this young girl raises the perennial question asked by the church and the world: "If God is so good, then why do bad things happen?" Think with me about the following story on minimum-wage jobs condensed from *The Wall Street Journal* and look again for signs of God at work in the world amidst the harsh effects of human freedom.

On payday, Brian Deyo's sole purchase is a $4.96 box of cheap bullets known as "full metal jackets." The bullets are purchased because he has little food on the table for his family of three.

Mr. Deyo works full time at a hockey-stick factory. He takes home $188.40 a week. After rent and utilities, that leaves about $20.00 for food—and no margin at all for misfortune, such as the one Mr. Deyo now faces. Vermont's brutal cold hit freakishly early this fall, and he must buy heating oil three paychecks ahead of time.

"Every day I'm making choices," says Mr. Deyo, who has a wife and a chronically ill two-year-old daughter. "Do I pay the rent and risk having the power cut? Or do we take a chance on both and buy food?"

This payday the choice is clear: He's two weeks late on the rent and the fuel tank must be filled. Unable to afford food, he will hunt for it. Stalking through the icy woods beneath the Green Mountains, Mr. Deyo mulls over his life. At age 28, he senses he has done something wrong. But he isn't sure what. "I'm proud to be a working man," the son of two factory workers says. "I only wish I made a living."

"Making work pay" has become a Clinton administration catch phrase, but one that appears increasingly hard to fulfill. Put simply, the aim is to lift working Americans above the poverty line—a threshold that Mr. Deyo and 9.4 million others currently don't reach. Almost 60% of poor families have at least one member working.

"Someone who plays by the rules and tries to work full time should be able to support a family," says Lawrence Katz, chief economist at the Labor Department. "But what is often obscured by policy debate is the sheer harshness of life in low-wage America."...

Barbara Stevens runs a crisis center in Newport, a town of 4,700 that is a two-hour drive from Burlington. The morning after the first big chill, her office was crammed with disheveled people unprepared for the winter and seeking help. Many were on their way to work. "They'd say things like "I've got two kids and no oil in the furnace, so we slept in the car last night with the heater on," Mrs. Stevens says.

One such visitor is Mr. Deyo, the hockey-stick worker. Late paying his bills, he has had his electricity disconnected several times. This is a special calamity for Mr. Deyo; his daughter has asthma and relies on a ventilator. Letters from Ms. Stevens and local doctors have helped him to get his power switched back on.

Ironically, Mr. Deyo is earning more that he ever has. After years of minimum-wage jobs, he now gets $5.50 an hour stencilling trademarks onto hockey-stick blades. But his annual gross income is so near the poverty line that now he qualifies for very little public assistance. In principle this suits him fine; he's a former National Guardsman and a conservative Republican wary of government and liberal "do-gooders." But in practice, just a minor setback—even a blown-out tire on his 1980 Buick—sets off a cycle of late bills, ruined credit ratings, and shaky employment.[3]

So where is God in all this, you ask? Signs of God's care clearly show in the existence of the news article itself, informing us of what is going on so that we are not in the dark. A light shines, and perhaps public opinion will begin to think more creatively about our present public assistance programs. Reformation always takes time.

God's help also shows in the daily help Mr. Deyo receives, and in the concern of more than a few dedicated public officials. Certainly we must do more, we could do more, and God expects more from us. But the laws are written by folks like you and me, and although God might work on behalf of a law that is righteous and fair for all, when we vote we vote freely, often favoring mostly ourselves.

Tears Like Bloody Sweat:
The Powerlessness of God

With issues like these on the table, what can Christian theology say to someone like Brian Deyo, as well as to the rest of us, particularly when people around the world wonder, "If God is so good, why do these terrible things happen?"

The expectation that God will stop human greed and the abuse it causes may arise from a highly idealized picture of an all-powerful God, not unlike early childhood pictures of all-powerful and all-caring parents. Some of this thinking is also influenced by traditional church teachings that God is

— *omnipotent (all powerful),*
— *omniscient (all knowing),*
— *omnipresent (everywhere), and*
— *infinite: meaning always and forever.*

These descriptions do point toward the truth of who God is, but when they are simply applied to God without other considerations, they are more deceptive than helpful. But because our childhood and adolescent pictures of God as a super-parent are too seldom evaluated from the biblical perspectives of freedom and sin, many of us simply continue to assume that because mom and dad were more powerful than we were, knew everything (or thought they did!), seemed to be always around (had always been and would always be), God will be the same way forever. Modern church growth research shows that many of the folks who drop out of church do so because their childhood images of God do not hold up in their adult years.

Although it may come as a surprise, the idea of God's self-limitation, or powerlessness, provides a helpful snapshot of the relationship of sin, freedom, and God's love for us. This idea has been valuable to theologians as far apart as Dietrich Bonhoeffer in the twentieth century and the Cappadocian Father, Gregory of Nazianzus, in the fourth.[4] In the Bible, the idea of God's powerlessness first shows in the encounter among Adam, Eve, and the serpent in the early chapters of Genesis. Eve and Adam were free to listen to God, but they chose to listen to another, and in the moment of their decision God was powerless. Jesus himself offers a view of the powerlessness of God when, shortly before his crucifixion, he weeps over the destiny of Jerusalem.

God of course is not ultimately powerless, a point made on every page of the Bible. But because of God's respect for human freedom, and because of what we Christians call sin—our refusal to listen to God's conversation—the notion of the powerlessness of God catches a bit of the breadth of God's love in a way that talk of God's power cannot.

So what has the powerlessness of God to do with the plight of a young girl on the streets of Louisville and a small family in the mountains of Vermont? Just this: God does not want such things to happen and is always working to make the world a safe place for all of us. Because our being made in the image of God leaves us free to make all kinds of decisions, including many self-centered ones, God does not intervene in the moment of decision. Instead, God works in a variety of ways to bring the world and all of us to our senses. Some might say this way of God is not terribly effective, and because of it too many suffer, but suffering comes from the way we use the freedom God has granted us.

The cartoon by Bil Keane below also makes this point. We might well wonder at the numbers of harsh things from which every one of us is delivered every day even though we were unaware of the danger.

》 The church and the world often raise hard questions about the relationship between suffering and God's love. But mission-minded Christians are not seduced from their basic posture of praise and thanksgiving.

When confronted with harsh realities, the notion of God's powerlessness in the face of human freedom provides a glimpse of understanding that often satisfies the immediate hunger to know more. In such fashion mission-minded Christians bring light to the dark places of the world.

Reprinted with special permission of King Features Syndicate

Questions
for Discussion

Developing the capacity to speak of God takes work, but it is a work much loved by mission-minded Christians. To strengthen *your* ability, use the following questions to discuss in a small group the stories about Mike Crawford, the newspaper girl, and Brian Deyo.

1. Which stories do you like best? What do they suggest about God that excites you? What do they suggest about God that confounds you?

2. How does your picture of God now differ from your childhood picture of God? How is it still like your childhood picture?

3. If you are part of a group of people using this chapter as a devotional or study guide, can you briefly share a personal story similar to those presented in this or the preceding chapters? And remember, when you tell the story it is not your life that you glorify, but the work of God in your behalf.

There is a fine line in Christian storytelling that must be acknowledged: does the story say more about you or does it say more about the majesty of God's action? Stories of godly praise and thanksgiving properly honor the latter focus. If this distinction is not clear, look afresh at the stories as models, and discuss the distinction as a group.

Chapter 4

STRESS AND BURNOUT

Losing the Joy

Highlights Maintenance attitudes generate chronic stress in both individuals and congregations. Whenever the church forgets Whom it serves and as a result is unable to celebrate the wonderful ministry of the Creator God, to that extent the church is isolated from its ministry and subject to stress and burnout. Theology makes a difference!

Lay leaders and other active church members are particularly vulnerable to stress. This shows whenever Christians say such things as:

— *"I just can't get the help I need."*
— *"There's too much to do and too little time to do it."*
— *"I can't take it any more."*

Like you, I have also heard of newcomers who, excited about life in a congregation new to them and seen as strong potential leaders, are all too quickly given a job that others did not want. Perhaps it was responsibility for a Sunday school class, or ushering at the door on Sunday morning, or providing volunteer help in the office during the week. And after a while they disappear.

These same jobs of course demand attention in mission-minded congregations. But because mission-minded Christians know that in all things God is mightily at work, jobs in these congregation are generally joined and shared with a spirit of expectancy. Attitude makes all the difference.

For clergy, chronic stress can lead to the involuntary termination of their ministry. In fact, all involuntary terminations of the pastoral relationship—and the trauma they visit on congregations—can be seen as the inevitable outcome of a maintenance mindset.

This chapter is written to help you think more realistically about the consequences of a maintenance mindset by showing its impact on individual Christians and congregations.

Signs of Dissatisfaction in the Congregation

Some of you by now may think that to develop a mission mindset all you have to do is tell your congregation what they need to do. But a mission mindset cannot be ordered or coerced, as is clear from the story of one minister who, having attended a seven-day conference on new approaches to leadership in the church, returned to his congregation and proceeded to tell them of *his* new vision for *their* ministry.

"I have a new vision for this church," he said, thinking he was acting on the teachings of the conference. The conference itself had, I later learned, covered all the right bases and addressed all the correct issues. But he simply had not gotten the message. He was what I call a captain of industry when he came to that conference, and he was a captain of industry when he left: he never realized that he had to work *with* his congregation to help them articulate the latent vision God had already developed in their midst, but which they needed help to voice.

» A mission-mindset cannot be ordered. If your vision for the ministry of the church is simply another set of rules and regulations to guide your congregation, your vision is mostly maintenance. It is not a mission-minded vision until it celebrates the work of God in your church and in the world.

Contrary to what one might think, a maintenance mindset does not guarantee a smoothly running church. Instead, it leads to a depressive church just as surely as it depresses the leaders in the church. Some of the following signs of dissatisfaction exist to some degree in every congregation and denomination, mainly because the church will never be free of a maintenance mindset. But the more this mindset dominates, the more these marks will show.

1. A maintenance mindset supplants good news with work news.

Maintenance-minded leaders tend to overvalue the ministry of the church. "We are the hands of God in the world," they say. Of course these leaders make a worthy point. But the way they put the issue implies that God is not much at work in the world. Instead of identifying and celebrating God already at work in the world—and inviting their people to join God in his ministry, maintenance-minded leaders push obligation and responsibility: law, not grace.

2. Current issues and exciting, relevant programs tend to drive maintenance-minded leaders.

Issues and programs are important in the church, of course. They help us focus our attention on what needs to be done in the service of God's righteousness—and to secure a more healthful world for all God's children. But even in this brief discussion the focus is on "us."

"But how could it be otherwise?" you ask. Think with me about alcohol and substance abuse and God's ministry in response. For years many congregations and denominations have been concerned about the issue of drunk drivers. But seldom does one hear the church celebrating the ministry of the One who, in response to this cultural disability, inspired the creation of such organizations as Mothers Against Drunk Drivers or Sons Against Drunk Drivers. And increasingly states are lowering the levels of blood alcohol at which a driver is judged legally drunk. Maintenance-minded Christians tend to celebrate events and organizations like these as expressions of the way human beings care for one another. Not so for mission-minded Christians. They know that in a sacramental universe the ministry of God deserves the greater celebration, for God is always working in our behalf.

3. As issues and programs are valued by the church, the authority of leadership becomes an issue.

In maintenance-minded congregations you often hear this refrain about church leaders: "Who do they think they are?" An adversarial relationship between leadership and the congregation begins to surface, a feeling that someone must be right and someone must be wrong. Gone is the celebration of God at work in the world.

4. A maintenance mindset encourages the development of an autocratic leadership style.

Convinced of the rightness of their views, scared of failure, defensive if their plans are not met with compliance, the tendencies of a tyrant begin to show. Leaders are too often forced by their own ideology into a defensive posture: "My way or no way." An imperial ministry shows.

5. As a result, a blaming attitude often exhibits itself.

"They (the congregation) aren't doing enough," say some. Members of the congregation also begin to hear more and more about what they *ought to do,*

should do, and

need to do

and little of the everyday, wonderful, and redeeming work of God in the world. Joy is the first casualty. Blame is its substitute.

6. With its focus on what leaders think ought to be done, members often feel left out in maintenance-minded congregations.

Then opposition and resistance to participation takes gradual but firm shape. As a result, maintenance-minded leadership becomes even more explicit about what ought to be done and needs to be done. An impasse develops.

7. Increasingly, the maintenance-minded leader trades essentials (identifying and celebrating the work of God in the world) for incidentals (a checklist of things to be done).

Take a look at many Sunday bulletins, weekly church newsletters, and denominational publications. They are full of what the church is doing and what the church ought to be doing, but not much appears about what God is doing in the world—aside from "calling" the church to more work.[1]

8. As a result of increasingly lengthy checklists, maintenance-minded leaders often fear that they sound like nags.

And they do. Because they are. With their commitment to tasks and projects and programs, the joyful celebration of God at work in our behalf is sacrificed. Furthermore, God is also perceived as a nag.

9. Maintenance-minded leaders also find themselves being treated as bearers of bad news.

With ever more work to be done and its successful completion seen as a sure sign of God's favor on their ministry, soon blame mounts and adversarial positions harden.

10. Constantly under pressure to get things done and obsessed with what has not been done, maintenance-minded leaders tend to forget to praise their people—and God.

Even while ushers show up every Sunday to faithfully perform their duties and Sunday school teachers faithfully engage their work, these leaders often bemoan the fact that still more don't participate. "Honey works better than vinegar" goes the old saying. Maintenance-minded leaders tend to be strong on vinegar.

» Using the signs of dissatisfaction outlined here, where does your congregation show the marks of a maintenance mindset?

Stress and Burnout
in Congregational Life

To the degree that "oughts" and "shoulds" characterize the life of any congregation, to that degree stress begins to show, mainly because God's ministry is now being dismissed in favor of "our" ministry. One might even say that stress accelerates to the degree that ecclesiology displaces theology in the church.

So what can be said of stress and burnout? Let's start with definitions.

Stress is a condition of strain brought about by an event or complex of events, and the strain compromises or disables our ability to cope with normal life demands. In short, stress is the human response to threat. Stress that is extreme and chronically generated produces burnout.

Burnout is a state of physical, emotional, and mental exhaustion marked by physical depletion and chronic fatigue. Feelings of helplessness and hopelessness show, and individuals and congregations suffering burnout develop a negative self-concept and negative attitudes toward themselves, life, and other people.

Now it must be noted that not all stress leads to burnout, and not all stress is bad. Stress has a positive side which also shows in congregational life. Research has discovered that low levels of stress can act as a motivator, and small amounts of it make us think better and help us move more quickly. One might say that all congregations benefit from some stress, the kind that helps us "rise to the occasion." One thinks here of the annual presentation of a much-beloved Christmas pageant, or a church choir community presentation, or an annual bazaar. Still, too much stress tips the scales the wrong way.

There is also an interesting connection between stress and illness, a connection that shows in the life of the church as well. The more stressed we are, the more likely we are to be sick—physically or emotionally. In fact, extreme and chronic stress in the life of any congregation leads to the development of a "sick" congregational life.

For the *congregation,* chronic stress tends to generate the disappointed and resistant member. For the *lay leader,* chronic stress tends to generate the dropout, on the order of "I've paid my dues and I can't do any more." For the *clergy,* stress generates despair ("We seem to be dead in the water") or an autocratic response ("I'll show them!"). At this point we are most likely on the way to an involuntary termination.

The "Guide to Stress in the Congregation" on the following pages illustrates further the signs of stress and burnout that appear when the focus of a congregation is on a maintenance mindset.

A GUIDE TO STRESS IN THE CONGREGATION:
THE EMERGENCE OF A MAINTENANCE MINDED ENGINE

Definition: *Stress is a condition of strain generated by an event or a complex of events. The more the strain increases, the more our ability to cope with normal life demands is compromised -- even disabled.*

As a member of a Christian congregation, fill in the "cloud" below with what you have been told you "need" to do, "ought" to do, or "should" do in order to be a faithful Christian. For lay and clergy leaders, fill in this cloud with what you believe your congregation "ought" to do and which they may not be doing. Drivenness and negativity are at issue here, as they are always in a maintenance minded engine.

1) As the church engages the world and the gospel, issues about what to do begin to show. Leaders work to clarify task and obligation, and labor to make peace between divergent, even oppositional views. The celebration of heavenly things suffers as earthly things are scrutinized.

STRESSORS

Works/Tasks, Oughts/Shoulds, Success/Failure: all substitute for a vision of God at work in the world.

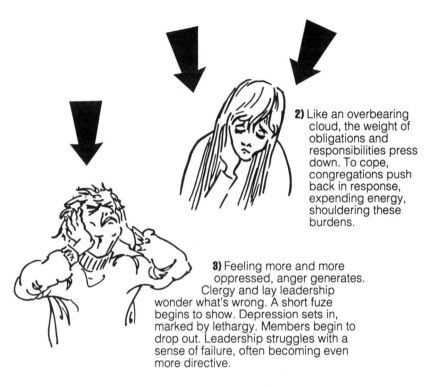

2) Like an overbearing cloud, the weight of obligations and responsibilities press down. To cope, congregations push back in response, expending energy, shouldering these burdens.

3) Feeling more and more oppressed, anger generates. Clergy and lay leadership wonder what's wrong. A short fuze begins to show. Depression sets in, marked by lethargy. Members begin to drop out. Leadership struggles with a sense of failure, often becoming even more directive.

4) Burnout shows when stress becomes chronic. Burnout is a state of physical, emotional and mental exhaustion marked by physical depletion and chronic fatigue, feelings of helplessness and hopelessness, the development of a negative self-concept and negative attitudes towards work, life, other people and God.

The Bottom Line: As church leaders become more directive in their leadership, focusing more and more on what the church "should" do and "ought" to do (often under the guise of a "challenge" - as if the law becomes any more palatable when differently framed), the life of the congregation becomes issue centered and leader driven. Adoration, praise and giving thanks to God take a back seat. By this point Christian congregations and their leaders are well into a perilous journey. A maintenance minded engine exacts a heavy toll.

The Shape of
Stress and Burnout

The ministry of the church in the world is broad and complex, so stress is to be expected. Building on the notion that "God so loved the world," all Christian ministry risks stress as faithful church leaders take it upon themselves to administer the work of organizations, to coordinate various tasks, to address issues deserving attention, and, indeed, to serve the world outside the church doors.

Consider the following three guides when diagnosing your own ministry and its attendant stress. Like a cloud of demanding witnesses, stressors always hover above a congregation and its leaders. So catalog your stressors.

1. Think about the stress generated by the organizations needing to be encouraged. "The youth group must have support." "The altar guild is not at all happy with the leak in the sink."

2. Catalog the myriad of tasks awaiting attention. "What are we going to do about the shelter for the homeless? We need to take some action, and it should have been taken yesterday."

3. What issues currently face you? "Parents are unhappy with the Sunday school." "We have got to get our heating and air conditioning bills under control."

So what can you do about the effect of all the stressors you currently face?

1. Take a close look at your attitude. Evaluate it carefully. Christians can see life as a series of problems or a series of opportunities: life as a glass half-full or a glass half-empty. Mission-minded Christians have learned to see opportunities not because life is particularly good or bad, but because God is always working in our behalf. It is a declaration of faith, isn't it, that God is at work in the world? And if God be for us, who can be against us? So with faith adopt an expectant mindset. A mission mindset goes a long way toward dismantling the power of oughts and shoulds and the pressure and loneliness they generate.

2. Remember that stressors are always with us. Acknowledging reality is a first step in dealing with it. Don't think that just because you are a Christian in the church of God you are immune to the stresses of life.

3. Make an inventory your stressors. Reconceptualize them in terms of God's ministry of making all things new. Ask yourself which responsibilities you can appropriately shoulder, and which you must delegate to others. Put first things first. Recognize priorities.

4. Learn to say no. Some things are simply too much to handle. Your plate can be too full. You can't be everyone's savior, although good-hearted Christian leaders too often get caught in this trap.

5. Talk things out with others whom you trust. Stress tends to isolate us, so a conversation about these things is particularly appropriate to break the isolation that stress naturally generates. The church has always worked best in council, or in communion with one another "when two or three are gathered together" in Christ's name.

The extreme and chronically generated stress generated by an overbearing maintenance mindset usually affects both congregations and individuals in the following patterns.

The Progression of Congregational Burnout

1. When unacknowledged, stressors weigh increasingly heavy, generating lethargy.

2. Members are boxed away from one another. A formerly healthy common life fractures.

3. More and more energy is spent "holding things together" or "keeping things balanced."

4. Personal edginess grows as the stressors demand the congregation's attention.

5. Anger begins to assert itself throughout the congregation.

6. The congregation divides into those who support current leadership and those who do not.

7. If not addressed, anger turns cold, becoming bitterness.

8. War accelerates. Congregational energy burns out.

When the ministry of the church becomes the primary focus of the church, *oughts* and *shoulds* predominate. Stress grows. The remedy is simply this: to begin afresh to celebrate the ministry of God in the world. Then all else tends to fall into place.

The Progression of Burnout in Individual Members

1. When unacknowledged, the stressors weigh increasingly heavy, generating lethargy.

2. Members are boxed away from one another. A formerly healthy common life fractures.

3. More and more energy is spent "holding things together" or "keeping things balanced."

4. Personal edginess grows as the stressors demand the individual's attention.

5. A "short fuse" syndrome begins to show.

6. Fatigue becomes a way of life. Church responsibilities are just "one more thing."

7. Stressed individuals begin to see the world from adversarial instead companionable perspectives.

8. Quiet depression generates, often showing as resistance and/or anger.

9. Enthusiasm and energy wane, a "Let them do it" syndrome takes shape.

10. Burnout begins to show. Members are now dropping out of active participation in the church.

The adversity generated by a maintenance mindset is not a pretty sight, yet it is a condition too often displayed in parish churches today.

Clergy are prime candidates for the stress generated by a maintenance mindset, and their patterns of stress are similar to those of congregations and individual members.

Patterns of Burnout in Clergy

1. If once God was close and they knew it, now a myriad of tasks, obligations, and expectations characterize their ministry. When asked to describe their weekly work, many clergy paint a picture of maintaining an institution. There is a pull toward tasks and programs.

2. A weariness begins to show. The shoulders sag a bit. There may be restless nights. "I don't have much to preach about this week," some say, or, "The board and I can't seem to get together on this issue."

3. Disappointed, they begin telling their people what to do, hoping that the generation of still more new programs will breathe excitement into the life of the church. By this point stress is giving way to burnout.

4. The good-hearted conversational ministry once enjoyed with their people—as together they first joined in ministry—gives way to a more autocratic style.

5. Pain spills over into family life.

The development of a mission mindset is not a cure-all to stress, and the tasks and church responsibilities will still need attention. But a mission mindset sets a context that puts these items in their proper place.

>> Think afresh about the shape of your ministry by considering the stressors in your life. Consider your vision of ministry. A fresh view of "who you are" can be a first step toward taking corrective action.

Involuntary Termination:
Bitterness Beyond Redemption

There was a time when the call to minister to a congregation was a call for life. Like a marriage, the relationship was for better and for worse—forever. Not so now. I hope the following discussion of the new phenomenon of involuntary termination of clergy will help both clergy and lay leaders assess a journey they want to avoid or fear they may already have embarked upon. For lay leaders in particular, if trauma is present in your congregation, the "Clergy/Congregation Relationship Map" on the opposite page can help you make a diagnosis and perhaps formulate a treatment.

The way in which a marriage between two human beings grows and matures—or not—sheds a lot of light on the way in which an involuntary termination also takes shape. A marriage is fundamentally a covenant relationship. And so is the relationship between a member of the clergy and his or her people.

Every marriage or covenant relationship can be laid out on the following continuum:

1. All marriages first begin as what can be called a *natural marriage*. Two people meet and a relationship is born. A covenant begins to take shape. Such "marriages" also begin to form as congregations interview many clergy for one position, although only one will "make it to the altar."

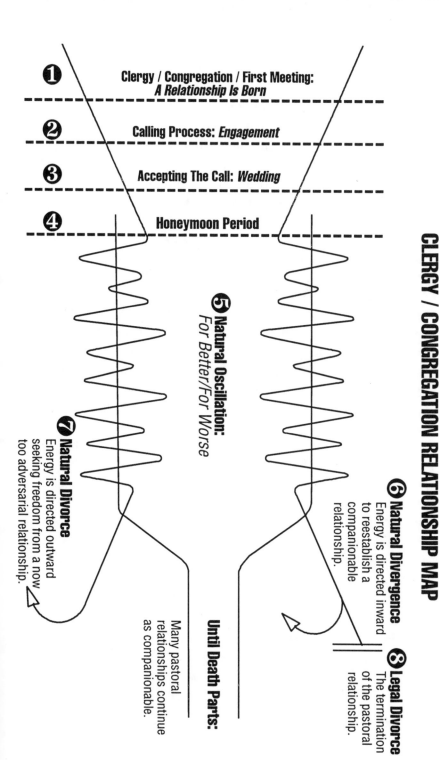

CLERGY / CONGREGATION RELATIONSHIP MAP

❶ Clergy / Congregation / First Meeting: *A Relationship Is Born*

❷ Calling Process: *Engagement*

❸ Accepting The Call: *Wedding*

❹ Honeymoon Period

❺ Natural Oscillation: *For Better/For Worse*

❻ Natural Divergence
Energy is directed inward to reestablish a companionable relationship.

❼ Natural Divorce
Energy is directed outward seeking freedom from a now too adversarial relationship.

❽ Legal Divorce
The termination of the pastoral relationship.

Until Death Parts:
Many pastoral relationships continue as companionable.

2. If there is promise in this new relationship, for couples a period of formal *engagement* usually follows. For clergy and congregations, further conversations take shape between themselves and calling committees that, if they hold substantial promise, move toward a "call."

3. Next the marriage of two human beings is made *legal* by a celebration of the covenant before God, the church, and the world. The marriage is celebrated with a wedding. For clergy and congregation, a call is issued by the congregation, accepted by clergy, and a new ministry celebration is held in the local church.

4. A honeymoon period ensues. For the most part in these early months neither spouse can do much wrong. Congregations and new clergy often share a similar period of time.

5. But time marches on. Months give way to a year or more, and since marriage is a covenant for better and for worse, for richer and for poorer, a *natural oscillation* also begins to show in the covenant relationship. By the time this marriage quality shows itself, the honeymoon is over. The principals, while moving in a mostly parallel track (as shown in the relationship map), from time to time move toward one another, and at other times move away from one another. For this reason many folks can rightly say that a marriage is never smooth.

In the same way that a natural oscillation characterizes every marriage, it also shows in the relationship between clergy and their congregations. This oscillation creates periodic expressions of both joy and disappointment. Life lived in covenant is for better and for worse, for richer and for poorer. Clergy and congregations are right to expect this, even welcome it as they stretch and grow in relationship to one another.

6. In the normal course of events, this natural marital oscillation turns into divergence. Hence, *natural divergence* is also a component in every relationship. What constitutes a

natural divergence? What signs does it show? A strong difference of opinion, a differing vision, different responses to the opportunities presented by life: all generate a natural divergence. Partners might feel somewhat "out of step" with one another, or "not on the same wavelength." Fearing that things are a bit more serious than just a "little spat," they might wonder about the possibility of some counseling help.

Anger begins to show as natural divergence takes shape. Anger of this sort is often redemptive. Indeed it is to be welcomed, for by its use covenant partners simply say to one another, "I miss you and I'm angry about it." Although unwelcome because of the discomfort it brings, a natural divergence is to be expected in most marriages, as well as in the clergy/congregation relationship. But a natural divergence is often the place where the hostile termination of the clergy/congregation pastoral relationship first begins. That is why recognizing it is so important, so that steps can be taken toward reconciliation. Otherwise, anger, or the fear of it, can push the principals still farther apart: "They don't understand." "She can't hear." "He won't listen." Battle lines are drawn. Positions harden.

7. *Natural divorce* takes shape when a natural divergence is not arrested. The spontaneous anger marking the time of natural divergence now changes to chronic anger. Increasingly the partners treat one another as adversaries. If, during the period of natural divergence, clergy and congregation still looked toward the relationship with some hope, now at a time of natural divorce they look outward for freedom. The relationship is well on its way toward dissolution.

By the time natural divorce begins to show in the relationship between pastor and congregation, positions are more intractably set, and at least one of the principals is now looking outside the relationship for new life. The theological idea of blasphemy offers a constructive insight into the power generated by a natural divorce.

Blasphemy can be conceived as chronic anger turned to bitterness. Tradition has it that blasphemy is the only unforgivable sin, simply because it is an attitude that no longer offers the possibility of conversation between God's Holy Spirit and human spirit. Without conversation a relationship can't be restored. Blasphemy is a function of human freedom, for, made in the image of God, human beings are free to destroy one another and themselves.[2] The more clergy and congregation strengthen their everyday relationship with bitterness, the less likely they are to listen to any possibility for redemption. Turning inward and choosing to see the world as each wants to see it, blasphemy consumes those caught in it as surely as night follows day.

8. Finally, *legal divorce* (or the termination of the pastoral relationship between clergy and congregation) will likely follow the development of a full-blown natural divorce.

Although most of the focus today is on the clergy who are affected by the involuntary termination of their ministry, in fact, lay leaders are often "terminated" as well. Here is how.

Most lay leaders are elected to positions of leadership by people who trust them. But what begins with much affirmation invariably undergoes a transition from honeymoon to real life—life for better and for worse. If lay leaders want only to please the congregation for the sake of personal affirmation, more and more they will feel pulled in all directions by the expectations of others. Resentment will grow, and a natural divergence will begin to show. As the inevitable differences in opinion begin to show between leaders and people, the style of leadership may become more autocratic, even distant or punitive. On more that one occasion I have heard lay leaders say something like, "If they [the congregation] won't do such and such, then there's no reason for us [the vestry or board or session] to provide this." Such relationships lead to a natural divorce as surely as the sun sets at night.

Redeeming the Prospect
of Involuntary Termination

If stress and burnout are developing into the termination of the relationship between you and your congregation, the following principles might help form for you a reasoned judgment about the possibility of redemption and restoration.

1. Relationship counseling is, at its best, a collaborative enterprise. If it is not collaborative, or cannot be because of the intensity of the trauma, it is likely to be unsuccessful. In other words, if natural divorce has taken firm shape, it is likely that the relationship cannot be redeemed.

2. If it seems that the expectations between you and your congregation are unclear, clarify expectations. You might make use of the relationship map to determine the growth of the divergence and the reasons for it. Rationality is helped by "seeing what is bothering us." This approach works well in the early stages of a natural divergence.

3. To test for natural divorce, look for intractable, glacial anger, and strong adversarial perspectives. All indicate that natural divergence is giving way to natural divorce. But by confronting your position as determined on the relationship map, you and your congregation can perhaps shock the relational system back to a more positive, conversational reality.

4. Know that the more positions harden, the more likely it is that you will be burdened with a highly idealized view of the relationship. On the one hand you and your congregation may believe things were much better than they actually were at the beginning, and on the other hand you and your congregation may believe that things are actually much worse than in fact they are at present.

5. If you serve as a consultant and make use of these guidelines, help the participants critique their idealized visions. Still, if blasphemy shows it may be too late for restoration.

Some congregations may be intractable in their commitment to a maintenance mindset. Having grown accustomed to maintenance thinking, they are not at all interested in changing. As a member of the clergy, if you are not content to work with this circumstance patiently, you should consider leaving before you burnout.

On the other hand, some clergy are intractably committed to a maintenance mindset. If you as a congregation are not willing to put up with this mindset from your minister, perhaps now is the time to commit to a separation.

Chapter 5

INSPIRATIONAL LEADERSHIP

Always a Celebrant

Highlights This chapter is written to help you think about your style of leadership in the church by seeing afresh the shape of effective ministry in today's church, and the kind of leadership you can offer to your congregation. It will describe various styles of leadership, including the captain of industry, the administrator/manager, the teacher and preacher, the liturgist/worship leader, and the counselor/caregiver.

You will then be offered an opportunity to consider another model, that of celebrant, and the special shape it takes:

— *Making the negative positive*
— *Expecting plenty, not scarcity*
— *Valuing diversity of opinion*
— *Possessing a vision of Christian maturation*
— *Giving thanks to God in all things*
— *Putting first things first*
— *Saying "thank you" to God and to the church*
— *Acknowledging that what we do matters to God*
— *Making criticism positive.*

The Shape Of Effective
Leadership in Today's Church

Effective clergy and lay leadership in today's church is marked by an ability to gather community. These leaders are able to help a collection of individuals become a congregation; they know who God is and the proper place of programs and issues in the life of the church.

But many of today's church leaders function another way. An article in *The Washington Post* reports that its city school board spends more time taking care of the business of the board than considering the education of the city's children:

> As one board member put it: "We concentrate on the business of the board as opposed to the business of the schools." Says another disappointed member, "I naively thought most of my time would be focused on educational issues like curriculum, testing, instruction, and teachers. But so much of my time is spent on how to repair a building, on personnel, on hiring practices." A consultant adds, "The boards of large school systems find themselves overtaken with noneducational, managerial and political issues."[1]

Does this tune sound familiar? Like this school board, many contemporary church leaders have been seduced into thinking that the first work of the church is taking care of the church: keeping buildings in repair, finding volunteer helpers for this task and that, and programming one thing and another. Members of board, sessions, committees, and vestries complain about a myriad of details. What is sacrificed is the capacity to identify and celebrate God at work in the world.

Think with me for a moment about why newcomers come to church in the first place. They don't come so they can help repair the roof or usher on Sunday morning. They probably come because they have been touched in some way by God, and they want to know a bit more about who God is. Encountered by a graceful coincidence or good fortune, they,

headquarters—have given up the mission-minded fervor that so splendidly marked their initial work in the church.

Far more important than organization is the way in which church leaders value God at work in the world. Leaders who are able to point out that the kingdom of heaven is at hand provide a strong gospel light for which many in the church and in the world hunger.

The Administrator/Manager

Leaders who define their style as one that stresses administration and management are good at organizing their church for ministry. But, unlike the captain of industry, a collaborative style often marks their leadership.

Leaders who value administration and management can be considered mission minded to the extent that they see and celebrate God's work in the church and in the world. But one doesn't find many of these mission-minded administrators in the church, mainly because the culture encourages them to value their ministry of management to an extreme. Their interests and biases tend to dominate, encouraging these leaders to value a smoothly running operation over mission. Substance gives way to form.

There is more to church life than management and administration, and invariably this style leads to a hunger for godly things that cannot be assuaged, no matter how well organized the body.

The Teacher and Preacher

This style of leadership would seem to welcome most naturally a mission mindset, and often it does. But even a passion for preaching and teaching can be overcome by the drive toward maintenance.

Leaders who primarily define themselves in terms of the teaching and preaching ministry of the church are often adept at highlighting responsibilities that "ought" to be addressed. Tending to function as nurturing parents, they may even call responsibilities "opportunities for service." But the enumeration of "work to be done" is a far cry from the vocation of identifying and celebrating God at work in the world.

You can also tell whether these leaders are given more to maintenance or mission by what they say in their sermons and in their teachings. If their sermons and teachings lay down the law about what ought to be done instead of celebrating what God is doing, and if the lay leaders are strong on calling church members to their "responsibilities," then what you have are teachers and preachers who are intent most of all on just keeping the work of the church going. If, on the other hand, the leaders who value responsibilities and obligations are even stronger in their estimation of God at work in the world, then they are mission-minded preachers and teachers.

The Liturgist/Worship Leader

In the main, this style of leadership centers around the altar of the church. Those finding themselves in this group figure that the single most important part of their ministry is that of presiding during times of congregational worship. All of the planning of the liturgy and preparations for worship can become seductive, though. Leaders who devote most of their energy to the work of selecting hymns, planning the pageantry, writing the prayers, and deciding what will go with this and that in the service can become detached from the daily life of the congregation or from thoughts of God at work in the everyday world.

Moreover, a strong need to control often accompanies the passion for liturgy. One such leader has described the function of the liturgy as the work of "bringing persons to uniformity in a common worship experience." No mention of God, but a strong note of control.

When carried to the extreme, this style so focuses on the heavenly realm that any connection with the earth is severed. Alert and appreciative about the way in which the liturgy itself reflects the glory of the divine, these leaders lose sight of divine glory in the midst of everyday life. Although called "celebrants" in the liturgy, often they forget how truly to celebrate.

The Counselor/Caregiver

Leaders defining themselves in terms of the work of a counselor and caregiver are often good at helping people in congregations feel better about themselves. Committed to a ministry of pastoral care, they tend to place a high value on contacts with individuals both in the church and in the community. Through excessive valuing of individual contacts, however, the life of the church as a community suffers. Although broken hearts may find solace with these leaders and greatly benefit from their care, counselors and caregivers tend to fracture the life of their congregation into many pieces.

A New Model of Church Leadership:
Always a Celebrant

The crisis in contemporary church leadership is a paradigm crisis, a crisis rooted fundamentally in the way the church itself understands ministry. But a new kind of leadership is beginning to show in the midst of contemporary church life. This new breed of leader values the nobility of the title "celebrant."

Seen also as strong leaders, the leadership they offer is not the muscular leadership of the captain of industry, nor does it focus too closely on administration, teaching, preaching, or the liturgy, nor does it overvalue the ministry of counselor and caregiver. These leaders are first of all celebrants of God at work in the world, a perspective that infuses the other five models with a power they sorely need.

» Compare the following picture of the leadership style of celebrant to your own style. What can you take away from this discussion that might make a positive difference in the leadership you offer the church?

Making the Negative Positive

From their certain hope that God is at work in the world, mission-minded Christians make every effort to reframe and reconceive every potential problem into an opportunity for celebration. This approach takes a bit of work, but the dividends are full of grace.

Based on an actual event, the following story reveals the spirit present in mission-minded leaders. Join me at a meeting of the finance committee of a mission-minded Presbyterian church.

Under new business, the executive for buildings and grounds announces that a leak had shown in the roof of the educational building.

"What a joy!" respond two mission-minded members of the board, a statement that blows the minds of the maintenance-minded Christians who are thinking, "How can this be? Are they out of their minds? How can any problem like that be anything other than tragic?"

In fact, mission-minded congregations and their leaders know that every problem provides a new opportunity for them to value afresh the faithfulness of God and their dependence on God's faithful help, always present and always near.

Maintenance-minded Christians, on the other hand, faced with news like this, immediately begin the task of assessing the damage, looking for revenue sources in the current budget or through the insurance company, or perhaps begin to think about raising money from the congregation. Deliberations in such congregations take the shape of wondering what the church

> *should do,*
> *ought to do,*
> *needs to do,*
> *even what God wants it to do*

with nary a word about the wonderful work of God bringing a leak to this board's attention.

Mission-minded Christians would eventually apply these same principles, but they would get to this place by a different route. For them, the opening response of "What a joy!" is simply an expression of the fact that 1) because the educational building truly belongs to God, they now have an opportunity to show their love in response; 2) now in the fullness of time the leak is no longer hidden, but out in the open; 3) God cares about the educational building and their stewardship of it; 4) as they deliberate they can expect God to open their eyes to new possibilities and resources perhaps temporarily hidden; and finally, 5) once again they are gifted with an opportunity to offer love afresh to God.

In the Christian church it is wrong to treat events like a leak in the roof or a problem in the church school or anything else as simply a problem to be fixed. That is the way of the world. Careful planning and execution have their place, but there is another way. Problems like these offer an opportunity to show our love for God.

> » The choice before us is always: Will we walk in the way of the gospel or the way of the world?

If you decide for the way of the world, know this: you are in company with much of the church, with its shrinking budgets, dwindling numbers, and dispirited attitude. If the gospel doesn't get your attention, maintenance will.

Does the church belong to God or does the church belong to us? Does the ministry of the church belong first of all to God or first of all to us? From the way many of us describe it, the church and its ministry are seen first of all as our own. God's participation is for the most part unacknowledged. Mission-minded Christians know otherwise, so even occasional adversity is put into a more heavenly perspective.

Expecting Plenty, Not Scarcity

A mile-wide streak of optimism characterizes celebrative leadership in the church. Now I don't mean to suggest that such leaders are pie-in-the-sky optimists. Though they are a hopeful bunch, their optimism is of course rooted in the steady confidence that God is always with us, and that, whatever they confront, God is already richly present and interested.

Mark Taylor and Carmen Berry, authors of the insightful book *Loving Yourself As Your Neighbor,* point out two basic attitudes about life revealed in the world and in the church. One they call an attitude of scarcity, the other they call an attitude of plenty. A maintenance mindset has an attitude of scarcity along the lines of

— *in life there is never enough to go around,*
— *if it is to be done I must do it, and*
— *no one is going to help out.*

An attitude of abundance develops from the certain knowledge that because God is at work in the world, and because God has our best interests at heart, far more beneficial things come our way than we ask for. Hence mission-minded congregations can even "welcome" a leak in the roof of the church.

Moreover, Taylor and Berry point out that this attitude of scarcity causes burnout in the church. Church members work harder and harder because "if it is to be done we must do it." Without much expectation that God *is* at work in the world, and unable to identify signs of God at work in the world, a certain loneliness develops. More and more the congregation reaches into its own resources. More and more energy drains away. Burnout inevitably results. Mission-minded congregations, on the other hand, able to identify God at work in the world and in their lives, see everyday life as a cup full to overflowing.

Now at this point you may well be wanting to say to me, "You exaggerate!" I do overstate the point, but only to make it more fully. You yourself know the attitude of scarcity that exists in the world and in your church, as well as the attitude of plenty that springs from the healthy expectation that because God is at work in the world, we also have every reason to be expectant and hopeful. And like me, I bet you know how easy it is to lean toward scarcity and away from an expectation of abundance. So does much of the church.

>> How does an attitude of plenty show in your leadership? How does an attitude of scarcity show? And what can you do about it?

Valuing Diversity of Opinion

Instead of seeing problems, mission-minded leaders tend to see opportunities for celebration. No matter how much pain there is, these ministers always look for signs of a loving God doing, in the midst of everyday life, infinitely more than they can ask or imagine. I don't mean to suggest that such leaders simply say "Be hopeful" when things are tough; that is shabby care. Rather, these men and women have learned that "joy comes in the morning." Because Another is also at work in the midst of life, they have learned to be expectant even when things look bleak.

Thus a difference of opinion at a board meeting, rather than generating fear of potential conflict, gives rise to a vision of the rich way everyone contributes to the whole. Instead of attempting to stop potential polarization when a difference of opinion appears, these leaders are glad to pause in the meeting to affirm the different ways in which so many faithful Christians are responding to the opportunity of ministry before them. Discussion is then cast into a more explicitly theological context. No longer will one group win and one group lose.

Now this way of thinking does not imply these leaders are naive. Indeed, the world is full of hostility, all of us are cantankerous at one time or another—some of us more so than others. But this reality does not diminish the validity of a hopeful approach to life and ministry.

A potentially divisive issue provides another illustration of a celebrative minister at work with her congregation.

At a meeting of the church executive committee, the main agenda item was a presentation of the architect's plan for a new sanctuary, and the committee's response was generally favorable. Discussion drew to a close, but suddenly one member of the board announced, "I just can't go along with all this. I haven't said much to this point, but I just can't remain silent any longer." He is strongly set in his views.

Without a second thought, the presiding pastor immediately announced, "Let's listen to Peter, because God may be speaking to us here. Please tell us what you're thinking, and maybe we can also help you put your thoughts into words."

She soon discovered what was upsetting him. The architect's drawings showed a building substantially larger than the present one, and older members like Peter were fearful they would lose some of the informality that they had learned to love on Sunday morning.

With no fear on her part about a contrary opinion or that a growing consensus might be shaken, the pastor carefully explained to the board that this was an opportunity to think even more deeply about God's invitation to consider the construction of a new building. The ensuing discussion exam-

ined a number of issues, and as a result the vestry directed the architect to return with plans that made better provision for informal conversation and fellowship in the new building.

As this story clearly shows, mission-minded committees are much less likely to fight because they believe that each member plays an important part in the overall discussion. For example, these boards and committees try to reach a consensus before putting an issue to vote. The consensus they work to develop could be one of unanimity, or it could be one of majority. These leaders also know, however, that consensus by unanimity can, on occasion, subtly coerce the minority to change its mind. Consensus by majority, on the other hand, because the board knows that a decision *will* be reached at some point, moves the board to value discussion itself as an opportunity to present many and various views. Each participant is seen and known as a faithful servant of God. But the consensus to which they move is one that, although a majority will reign, values the minority voice as a reminder that "we must be vigilant."

How often do your board or committee meetings sink to a win/lose conflict? It is a given that conflict can be brought about by personalities unable to conceive another way of operating. But for the most part, win/lose battles in the church are generated because leadership in the church no longer values differences of opinion as expressions of God's providence.

>> Lifting our vision to see God's ministry as one overflowing the cup of life with many possibilities will not bring about an end to conflict, but it does offer a certain hopefulness when knotty problems are considered.

Possessing a Vision of Christian Maturation

Strengthening the faith of Christians (and particularly adult Christians) stands at the center of a mission-minded congregation's common life.

The consequences of little or no adult education are two-fold. First, the interest of many mainline adult Christians wanes, and as a result more than a few drop out of church. And second, with no vision of the Christian life and witness, a maintenance mindset assumes a stronger shape in those who remain.

I've found that many adults drop out of church because their knowledge of God doesn't keep pace with the reality of their adult lives. For example, it is often difficult for adult or teenaged friends of a person killed by a drunk driver to keep faith if their knowledge of God is no wider than a first-grade Sunday school image of God as a heavenly, always-providing-good-things parent. No matter how legitimate this image is, it is not an adequate picture of a God who has chosen to love us, a God who respects our freedom even when we choose to destroy one another.

Part of the work of Christian maturation is setting ourselves to the task of broadening our childhood and adolescent understandings of God. In and of themselves there is nothing wrong with our early ideas, but adulthood demands a far richer belief in God than our early years provide.

How can any congregation become more intentional about the development of a sturdy Christian faith? What is it appropriate to expect? The author of the letter to the Hebrews picks up these questions when addressing the early church and the ministry to which it was committed:

> And what of ourselves? With all these witnesses to faith around us like a cloud, we must throw off every encumbrance, every sin to which we cling, and run with resolution the race for which we are entered, our eyes fixed on Jesus, on whom faith depends from start to finish: Jesus who, for

the sake of the joy that lay ahead of him, endured the cross, making light of its disgrace, and has taken his seat at the right hand of the throne of God. (Hebrews 12:1-3)

One might say that embracing Christian maturation is like a race. Certainly there is a goal toward which we work. But in mission-minded congregations, rather than leaving the development of a mature Christian faith to chance, church leaders are intentional about it.

The idea of being intentional when thinking about Christian maturation is an idea as old as family life itself. Children are not left at loose ends to discover and learn their family identity. In healthy families they are taught family principles: the history of the family, at least through the time of their grandparents, what their family believes about the world, and what it means to be a member of the human family in the trials and tribulations of the world. Mission-minded Christians are every bit as intentional about the nurture and growth of Christian faith.

In a similar way, the development of a strong and sturdy Christian faith ought not to be left to chance. With a clear vision of the shape of Christian maturation, clergy leaders will preach it, pray it, and teach it. So will lay leaders, particularly if the whole of the congregation knows what is the focus. As a result, both leaders and congregation will have a clearer idea about Whose they are and the fundamental shape of God's—and their—ministry in the world. With this kind of common life, one can only say that the kingdom of heaven is truly at hand.

Giving Thanks to God in All Things

Perhaps you are wondering about other ways to help your congregation develop more of a mission mindset. Here is a suggestion. Whenever gathering for business, spend a portion of your time listening to God through Scripture and com-ing to God in prayer. The power of Bible study and prayer cannot be underestimated.

You might also use two questions as a way to "get on board" after having been apart from one another for a while:

1) What wonderful blessing has come your way since we last met?

2) What happened to you since we last met that you hope will never happen to you again?

These two questions in particular offer an opportunity for committee members to catch up with one another after a time of separation, and they encourage a brief time of sharing.

But I also know that some of you, reading this far, might be saying something like, "I can't expect my people to take to Bible study this quickly. For them Bible study and boredom are closely synonymous." I know this is too often true, and that Bible study and reflection, along with prayers of thanksgiving, are best introduced slowly and sensitively. But even without Bible study, the two questions I've suggested will go a long way toward helping your people become more aware of the presence of God in their lives.

> » Mission-minded Christians are able to give thanks in the midst of a complex, puzzling, and confusing world because they know they are not alone in the world. God is always close, working in behalf of the world. Hence, no matter how bleak things may look, mission-minded Christians look up with expectation and thanksgiving.

Putting First Things First

Business meetings in mission-minded congregations begin like meetings in every congregation: first there is a call to order. But after a call to order, the route of business takes a different twist.

Maintenance-minded Christians begin their meetings by looking backward—to the secretary's and treasurer's reports, and then on back to unfinished business and old business before they finally turn to new business.

Mission-minded Christians, on the other hand, want to look forward as prayerful, worshipful Christians. So their call to order is often followed with prayer, brief Bible study, and personal reflection, perhaps using the two questions previously noted. Then the first business on the table is new business. Not old business. Not unfinished business. New business.

Mission-minded Christians, you see, know that vision is the business of the church. So leaders in these forward-looking, gospel-living congregations often delegate the reports of the treasurer and the secretary to an executive for action prior to the business meeting, trusting the executive committee to find the ways and means to introduce items needing attention. Now, with newfound time, business meetings in mission-minded congregations spend their opening minutes thinking afresh about God's work in their midst, in their community, and in their world. They identify God at work in these places, they lift it up for praise and thanksgiving, and then they seek to determine how they can best join in God's ministry.

"So why," perhaps you wonder, "do Christians spend so much time at the beginning of every meeting on the secretary's and treasurer's reports if they hate them so much?" The answer is easy to discern. Many Christians are honored to be elected to positions of leadership in the church and they commit themselves to addressing the maintenance of the church with deep care and respect. So, with much enthusiasm these folks get right to the task, spending all sorts of time and energy over the five-dollar overage in office supplies, and whether this or that was said at the previous meeting. After several meetings, like others before them, these leaders too find board and vestry meetings less than satisfying. To avoid this pattern, try these suggestions:

1. Announce at the beginning of your meeting that God is at work and interested in the world. Prayer celebrating God at work in the world is a good way to begin.

2. Next, identify God at work in both your congregation and in your local community. For example, you might have heard that the mayor or board of governors has identified the need for a new road, or the provision of shelter for the homeless, or the repair of the local school. For mission-minded Christians these deliberations show the work of God in the world, and the natural response is one of adoration, praise, and thanksgiving.

3. With signs of God's ministry now on the table, declare your solidarity with this ministry by means of prayer, or perhaps with monetary support. Paul's understanding of Christ's headship in the church (Eph. 1:22; 4:11-16; Col. 1:18) is a helpful concept. As church leaders we may be of several minds about what matters in the world and what the church ought to do in response, but by actively listening to God and considering God at work in the world, we are more likely to become of one mind as we begin to know the mind of God.

Saying "Thank You" to God and to the Church

The life of a mission-minded congregation is marked with praise and thanksgiving, an attitude displayed every time they meet. Maintenance-minded congregations, on the other hand, tend to take one another for granted. Because they expect one another to do what they "ought" to do, those who are maintenance minded don't often feel constrained to say words of thanks.

For example, many mission-minded clergy at the time of announcements make it a point to praise members of their congregation not only for their work in the church but about their work in the world. Inspired to offer thanks for a member or a group during worship on Sunday morning and, fearful of forgetting, they may pause at a convenient time and, without interrupting the flow of worship, offer in that moment praise and thanksgiving for the life and ministry of one of God's children.

Ample opportunities to offer praise and thanksgiving show themselves in the church. One can give thanks for the Sunday morning work of the ushers, the ministry of members of the altar guild, Sunday school teachers who regularly give of their time and talent to the life of the church, parents who commit to bringing their children to church, the choir who offer their gift of music, and church committee members who serve faithfully. Everyone has an opportunity to exercise a ministry of praise and thanksgiving on Sunday morning, or in the weekly bulletin and monthly newsletter.

In maintenance-minded congregations, announcements on Sunday morning are designed to apprise members of new opportunities for service and new obligations. Indeed, Christians do have responsibilities and obligations in the world, but the church too often values responsibilities and obligations—work news—more than good news. The choice is yours.

THE IMPORTANCE OF PRAISE & APPLAUSE IN THE CHURCH

The development of a celebrative Christian community is much helped by leadership paying close attention to affirmation and affection. Inspiration is at issue here.

Praise and thanksgiving often suffer when church leaders pay too much attention to reminding members of their several responsibilities, telling them what they ought to do and should do, challenging them to greater efforts, at the expense of affirming signs of grace clearly present in their lives.

The first step in developing a mission minded engine is that of celebrating God's presence and ministry in the midst of life: the second step is the celebration of the faithful response of the people of God to God's initiatives.

101 WAYS TO PRAISE A CHILD

Wow • Way To Go • Super • You're Special • Outstanding • Excellent • Great • Good • Neat • WELL DONE • Remarkable • I Knew You Could Do It • I'm Proud of You • Fantastic • Superstar • Nice Work • Looking Good • You're On Top of It • Beautiful • Now You're Flying • You're Catching On • Now You've Got It • You're Incredible • Bravo • You're Fantastic • Hurray for You • You're On Target • You're on Your Way • How Nice • How Smart • Good Job • That's Incredible • HOT DOG • Dynamite • You're Beautiful • You're Unique • Nothing Can Stop You Now • Good for You • I Like You • You're a Winner • Remarkable Job • Beautiful Work • Spectacular • You're Spectacular • You're Darling • You're Precious • Great Discovery • You've Discovered the Secret • You Figured It Out • Fantastic Job • Hip, Hip, Hurray • Bingo • Magnificent • Marvelous • Terrific • You're Important • Phenomenal • You're Sensational • Super Work • Creative Job • Super Job • Fantastic Job • Exceptional Performance • You're a Real Trooper • You Are Responsible • You Are Exciting • You Learned It Right • What an Imagination • What a Good Listener • You Are Fun • You're Growing Up • You Tried Hard • You Care • BEAUTIFUL SHARING • Outstanding Performance • You're a Good Friend • I Trust You • You're Important • You Mean a Lot to Me • You Make Me Happy • You Belong • You've Got a Friend • You Make Me Laugh • You Brighten My Day • I Respect You • You Mean the World to Me • That's Correct • You're a Joy • YOU'RE A-OK • My Buddy • You Made My Day • That's the Best • A Big Hug • A Big Kiss • Say I Love You! Remember, a smile is worth 1,000 words!

—via St Dunstan's Church, Tulsa, Oklahoma

THE ANGLICAN DIGEST
MICHAELMAS A.D. 1992

Acknowledging That What
We Do Matters to God

Celebrative leaders also acknowledge the way in which their people help God take care of God's world in their daily occupations. These leaders know full well that the life of every community would be impoverished without secretaries, moms, dads, electricians, plumbers, nurses, business executives—the list goes on and on. Every Christian has an important part to play in helping God take care of the world. In these communities, through acknowledging their daily work, Christians have learned to value that work as important ministry—no matter what it may look like in the eyes of the world.

Mission-loving Christians believe that, in the same way a shepherd balances the needs of each of the sheep against the welfare of the flock, God converses with us about the jobs that we decide to take. Indeed, there is a direct connection between our daily work and what the Christian church calls "ministry." And this notion departs from the common belief that ordained clergy are the only ones who have a ministry, while everybody else just works. That is why mission-loving leaders often take time during the time of Sunday morning announcements, in the weekly bulletin, or in the church newsletter to recognize by name Christian saints and their daily work.

Making Criticism Positive

In a broken world and in a broken church, from time to time tough words about things that matter need to be said, but more than a few church leaders fear holding others accountable for their actions. "I don't want to hurt their feelings," they might say. So by ignoring the problem still others suffer, and leaders are left with guilty feelings about what they should have done but have not done.

Still other church leaders take a "hard-nosed" stance when criticism is deserved. They say too much and their words are too hard. Then hurt feelings spread all around, rippling out into the life of the community like troubled waters.

In fact there are times to set limits on others, holding them accountable for their actions—or lack of action. But one must remember, the people of God in congregation are not employed. They are present as folks called by God into community. Hence, holding Christians in community accountable for their actions ought to be marked with sensitivity and consideration—not at all a bad way to approach life generally.

Some basic principles are in order:

1. If a word about performance or boundaries or attitude deserves to be given, set a private time to talk about it. And don't discuss or set the time while in a public place.

2. State right away the reason for the meeting. This is best done when the meeting date is first arranged. But if it is not done then, it should be done as soon as the meeting commences.

3. Be specific about exactly what is troubling you, and talk only about that. Times and dates are appropriate, and a clear recapitulation of the failure. It might have been the lack of a follow-through on a committee recommendation, or the scheduling of duties, or an off-putting manner leaving others "cold." If there is other material about which you have not spoken, perhaps because you were "saving" it, leave it alone. It should have been said some time ago.

4. Give the person with whom you are talking an opportunity to set the record straight. Encourage his or her side of the story. Expectations may have been unclear, there may have been family or business crises that interfered, or perhaps it is a personality pattern that could be changed.

5. Keep your tone of voice and body language neutral. Don't belittle or chide; this is demeaning. Encourage them to do most of the talking, but don't leave them hanging without a response. We are talking here about a consultation and a conversation, not a monologue.

6. Close the meeting with praise and with a plan for the future. And assure them that this issue is now closed.[2]

There is a time to set limits and to become clear about expectations, and mission-minded Christians seek to do it with grace. Even when faced with the likes of a cantankerous curmudgeon—and there are many of us in the world—mission-minded Christians don't like to make war. Their approach is a far cry from one member of the clergy who, in a public disagreement with a member of his congregation that should have been settled privately, observed that he would be around to preside at her funeral!

Questions
for Discussion

1. What ideas in this chapter most interest you? Why? Interest and enthusiasm always indicate a movement from one thing to something else, on the order of moving from boredom to life. What visions of leadership are you moving from and to?

2. Which of the first five descriptions of leadership styles (excluding the one of the celebrant) paint the most accurate picture of your style? There is likely to be a combination, on the order of thirty percent of this one, sixty percent of that one, and ten percent of another one.

3. Every Christian is a celebrant to some degree or another. And even if the posture of celebration might have been drawn more sharply in the first-century church, there are notes of celebration in every Christian congregation today. What ideas in the discussion of the leader as celebrant interest you, and how might you begin to incorporate these perspectives into the leadership you offer?

4. Sadly, if you do not attend to the important ministry of helping the church identify and celebrate God's work in the world, a mission-minded celebration will not likely take place in your congregation. How might you as a congregation begin this work?

Chapter 6

LEARNING TO SING THE SONG OF ANGELS

Becoming a Celebrative Congregation

Highlights The following discussion pictures a mission mindset at work in the life of two congregations. You will read about clergy and lay leadership, and the part both play in developing the spirit common to these congregations. You will also see the importance of *intentionality* on the part of leadership in the development and nurture of this mission mindset. Mission-minded leaders don't simply hope and pray this way of thinking will develop: they help it take shape.

You will find in this chapter ideas to help you refocus your congregation's vision of ministry. But remember this point: you can "push" any new vision for ministry but it will only give expression to a maintenance mindset. Indeed, it will simply be only one more task to complete. The law by any other name is still the law.

A mission mindset is not contrived. It springs from the hope that God is at work in the world and is revealed in the celebrative care offered to congregations by their leaders. I hope you will read the following two illustrations looking for the spirit of this enterprise. Compare and contrast what was done with what you might do. As a result, you might find in these stories some of the refreshment and vision for which you may be looking.

Cornerstone United Methodist: Celebrating the Presence of God

Welcoming her people to worship on a recent summer Sunday, Gail Ford Smith, pastor of Cornerstone United Methodist Church in Houston, Texas, announced that a new opportunity to serve God had presented itself during the previous night. The rains of tropical storm Arlene, still pouring off and on as she spoke, had produced a leak in the roof of the sanctuary. Some of the overhead lights had also shorted out.

With a clear note of hope and celebration, Pastor Smith reflected on the idea that the leak had provided a special opportunity to respond to the generosity of God. The leak was a gift! And she was serious. Her congregation laughed as she spoke, but it was not laughter at the absurd.

Although this part of her announcements took no more than a minute or two, the spirit of celebration continued as this pastor helped her congregation think about the Father's Day picnic still scheduled for later in the afternoon, although it would be moved to inside the fellowship hall.

Depressed leadership is going to develop a depressed congregation. Compulsive leadership is going to develop a compulsive congregational life. Celebrative leadership is going to generate a celebration. What would you do about a leak in the church roof? Praise God for the gift of opportunity, or moan, "Isn't it awful?" The former generates praise and hope, the latter offers despair.

>> The attitude of leaders makes all the difference in the life of a congregation.

The Importance of Saying "Thanks"

These words of praise and celebration were not limited to the announcement period on this particular Sunday, or just to Pastor Smith. The chair of Cornerstone's Pastoral Concerns Committee, also lay reader for the day, spontaneously prefaced his reading from Genesis by remarking on how Cornerstone's common life was being much enriched by their minister, newly returned from a conference meeting. "You have brought us to a place of joy," he said, contrasting their current life to the depressed spirit of the church before she came to be their pastor.

"During this first year," says Gail Smith, "all my sermons have had an underlying theme of God's graceful acceptance and his joy in working with us. I write tons of thank-you notes every Monday morning, and I try to lift up in everything I do the wonderful work God is doing in our midst." Can you begin to see why this congregation is undergoing healing and a renewal?

> » One cannot underestimate the importance of saying thank you and offering praise for work well done. It is crucial for a healthy congregational life, and it must be done consistently and extravagantly.

People in mission-minded congregations don't praise one another just because it is a good thing to do (which it is), but because, simply knowing they are children of God and loved by God, they give thanks to God and for one another in all things.

Mission-Minded Preaching

But Pastor Smith was not yet done this day. A spirit of celebration showed itself in her sermon as well. Preaching on the story of Abraham, Hagar, and Sarah and the tension that began to develop between Sarah and Hagar as two heirs began to lay claim to the blessing God gave to Abraham (Genesis

21:8-21), this preacher moved from the natural selfishness always at work in the world to the *presence of a loving Father in the world* (it was Father's Day!) who provides more than enough for all of us. Here she joined the Genesis passage with the companion lectionary text from Matthew (10:24-39), the story of Jesus speaking about the sparrows of the air, and how much God provides even for them. God is, Pastor Smith concluded, truly a "heavenly" Father, always blessing us with bounty.

This kind of preaching is precisely why the people of Cornerstone can celebrate even a leak in the roof. Gail Ford Smith's sermon was presented in what I have learned to call a "kingdom-of-God" format—on the order of "The kingdom of heaven is at hand...," which of course it always is, a point missed by preachers preaching work news sermons. With sermons and leadership like this, one can clearly see why congregations like Cornerstone United Methodist Church are rapidly growing in spirit and numbers.

» Mission-minded, celebrative sermons are clearly focused on God at work in the world, not the works of the church in the world. The former celebrate good news, the latter work news.

Developing a Welcoming Community

Many computer programs are marketed today on the basis of their being "user friendly." One also hears talk in church growth circles about "user-friendly" congregations and "user-friendly" worship. Without making too much of this term but also recognizing the importance of hospitality, mission-minded congregations pay attention to the ways in which they receive and welcome newcomers.

Pastor Smith and her congregation are committed to presenting the gospel in as welcoming a fashion as possible, and they begin in the parking lot. In fact, when Gail Smith first came to Cornerstone, the four most prominent places in the church parking lot were guarded by concrete posts welcoming only church staff. With the consent of the congregation's leaders, these spaces are now designated for the visitors God is always bringing to God's church.

> » Developing a welcoming community life is not only a good thing to do and a worthwhile element in any plan to bring the gospel to the world: it also expresses the love of God that is always reaching out for us.

Welcoming others expresses the love of God in a way that satisfies the hunger of God's children to find a place of peace on earth. So now this question: How do you present the gospel to those who are among you for a first time? Make up a list of the ways, and then reevaluate them.

Taking Risks

As this is written, Gail Ford Smith has been pastor of Cornerstone for a little more than a year. In this year Cornerstone's previously declining budget has not only stabilized, but pledges have increased. And even with what some would consider an overwhelming debt maintenance on the new physical plant and a tight budget, the board of Cornerstone recently voted money to replace the worn-out carpet in their multipurpose sanctuary so that it would be more welcoming to younger members. "The money will be there," they said. And at this point there is no reason to believe otherwise. The pockets of God are deep, and particularly so in celebrative communities like this one.

What is happening at Cornerstone United Methodist Church is not isolated to a few congregations in the American church. Nor is it isolated in only one or two denominations. Celebrating congregations are increasingly showing in American churches, and their celebrative attitude is not contrived. They celebrate because they know God is at work in the world and in their lives, and every Sunday they sing a song of joy that sends an occasional shiver down the spines of its members.

St. Peter's-in-the-Woods:
Expecting God to be Present

In my previous book, *Church Growth and the Power of Evangelism,* I introduced you to St. Peter's-in-the-Woods, a new Episcopal church located in densely populated western Fairfax County in northern Virginia. Almost from their beginning I was privileged to be part of their journey while they searched for a permanent minister during their first year. The following narrative paints a more complete picture of the way a celebrative theology fuels the engine of parish life.

St. Peter's began at the urgings of the rector of a neighboring Episcopal church. As a result of prayer and meditation (including a retreat for those who were thinking with him about establishing this mission congregation), thirty members chartered the church. A description of the property on which they planned to build was included with their patron's name, hence, St. Peter's-in-the-Woods.

> » A prayerful attitude always marks the center of a mission-minded congregation's life. Christians in these congregations expect God to be present in the midst of life.

The Possibility of Growth

From the time of its first public meeting, this congregation began to grow. Meeting at the Bonnie Brae elementary school fourteen months later, St. Peter's numbered around one-hundred-sixty active members, an extraordinary rate of growth. Where their Sunday school at first numbered less that ten children, in less than a year it numbered thirty-five, and more than fifteen teenagers regularly gathered for youth group meetings.

How did such growth happen? Even though their area of northern Virginia was already full of established neighborhoods, the leaders of St. Peter's focused their attention on several crucial areas of ministry, not the least of which was the joyful celebration of God working a miracle in their midst:

— *the quality of worship on Sunday morning*
— *the welcoming of newcomers*
— *the importance of publicity*
— *the development of an effective Sunday school*
— *the formulation of a coffee/fellowship hour*
— *the explicit encouragement of its members to celebrate the presence of God.*

At St. Peter's these areas were valued according to how well they gave expression to God's aggressive love in the world. Always we ask this question: How is God at work in these events, and how can we best offer support to God's work?

》 Effective leadership in today's church pays close attention to the full range of congregational life. With intentionality everything is evaluated.

Worship: Singing the Song of God's Love

From the beginning, worship on Sunday morning was an event to which St. Peter's looked forward. They knew that in church on Sunday morning they would hear about God at work in the world, and find there the encouragement to come afresh to the throne of grace. The doors to the universe were opened wide on Sunday morning.

With their encouragement I also took it upon myself always to look closely for God at work in the world and in their common life, and then I offered to St. Peter's what I saw. I did not do this alone for long, however. For example, on one occasion the chair of the publicity committee was in a stew about his failure to get a general mailing out to the community inviting their attendance to worship on Easter Day. As we talked, it became clear to us that in his plight God was giving the entire congregation an opportunity to stuff envelopes. So after the last hymn and with joy, every member who could stay remained to stuff four thousand envelopes. It took only a few minutes. God is good and in that moment we knew it afresh.

We at St. Peter's also paid attention to the way the Bible was read in public worship, the way in which lay and clergy officiants presided at worship, even the way we sang—or did not sing. All of us can't sing like angels. Donn Starry, a member of St. Peter's, admitted that he couldn't sing a note, but he hums well, and while I was there Donn hummed with joy. Instead of a quiet drone when hymns are sung, mission-minded leaders and their congregations sing (or hum!) like there's no tomorrow. They also sing because they have been encouraged and enabled to sing, and because they are seriously touched with the belief that God is close.

Remember the advice about the importance of clear and intentional leadership noted in this chapter's highlights? Mission-minded congregations and their leaders know that if God's ministry is to be truly recognized, the whole of the congregation must be reminded of it at all times and in all places. Intentionality about the celebration is crucial. Most congregations go wrong by simply assuming that Christians will naturally remember the wonderful but invisible presence of God in the world. Not so.

A Praying People

As St. Peter's learned more and more to value the ministry of saying "thank you" to God, we also continued to encourage one another to celebrate God's ministry in the world by giving it constant voice. For example, Dan Danford, who was senior warden at the time, is one of those wonderful Christians who always listen for God when church decisions have to be made. Dan opened our meetings with sensitive and personal prayer and he led them in the same way. When appropriate, Dan also invited those present to expect God to provide the help we needed when sharp issues asserted themselves. And at still other times Dan, like others in the congregation, was known to tell stories about God at work in the world. Our common life was always a celebration.

>> The mission mindset likes the task of telling stories about God at work in the world. When leaders model the importance of prayer, the whole of the congregation learns to identify God at work and to share through prayer and praise what God is doing in their lives.

Welcoming the Stranger

As a new congregation, St. Peter's placed the greatest of importance on the welcome of newcomers. Every time a visitor graced our door we were fully aware that they were a gift from God. St. Peter's also had become aware that as many as nine-tenths of the visitors on Sunday who are called upon the same day by a member of the parish become active members. If they are visited several days later, or not until the following Sunday, the numbers will drop considerably. A half-hearted welcome on Sunday causes the kind of quiet disappointment that shows up in the statement, "Let's try someplace else next week."

But because of the many responsibilities generated by the start-up of a new congregation, and because my part-time leadership did not allow me to provide this visitation ministry, St. Peter's constructed a telephone ministry to reach out to those God brought to us. This is how they did it.

Greeters at the door of St. Peter's identified every newcomer. During my tenure it was not unusual to see two of our official greeters spot an unfamiliar face entering the front door and with joy respond: "Now there's somebody I don't know!" They would immediately greet the visitors with a smile and an outstretched hand. Both of them knew who brought these visitors to church.

Next, our visitors were introduced to others who came to sit with them, and this welcome was followed by a telephone call made within thirty-six hours to express joy at their visit. The call was also designed to find out:

1) How did things go on Sunday morning?

2) Did you feel welcome?

3) Did we leave anything undone that should have been done?

4) Do you have any questions that I can answer now?

5) Will you worship with us again?

With this kind of care on Sunday morning and with the follow-up procedure just described, we were retaining in some months better than seventy percent of those who visited us. And in our follow-up telephone calls visitors would make remarks like: "You're so friendly," and "I've never heard a congregation talk so openly about God."

>> No matter what plans you make to welcome these guests from God, know this: mission-minded congregations make it clear that God is in charge.

Welcoming these visitors on Sunday morning means singing the song of God at work in the world. So what does such a welcome sound like? Perhaps something like this: "God is with us, and we are overjoyed to see evidence of God's love again this morning. We are delighted to welcome those of you visiting with us, for we know that you have been brought by God. So in God's name we are honored to welcome you."

To assist with this ministry of welcome and inclusion, and because we knew that God needed our help as he worked quietly in our midst, everyone at St. Peter's made a commitment to wear nametags on Sunday—even lay readers and clergy. We knew that the more intentional the church could be about community building, the more likely it was that community would form. God creates all kinds of opportunities for communion. God is a communion-building God, and the use of nametags greatly enables this ministry.

Now I know as well as you do that nametags are a bother to many. And some might simply say, "I don't want to wear one. I know everyone already." But in fact not everyone does, and newcomers will be literally left in the dark. God wants it otherwise. Seldom if ever do mission-minded Christians have to hear that "Nametags ought to be worn" or "should be worn" or "need to be worn." More than hearing from their leaders what they ought to do and should do, mission-minded Christians hear about the wonderful way nametags serve God's ministry. And so, with grateful hearts, they act in response. Always before us is the choice: work news or good news, maintenance or mission.

The Ministry of Publicity

The welcome of newcomers also led St. Peter's to value the ministry of community publicity. Weekly announcements in the local newspaper and community newsletter kept our presence before the public, so that whenever someone thought about going to church for the first time, they would be likely to remember "that ad." In this same vein, the yellow pages in our local telephone book were also valued as a resource.

We also found that signs placed throughout our community produced excellent results. Late every Friday afternoon members of St. Peter's placed eighteen portable signs in the communities and shopping centers adjacent to the Bonnie Brae Elementary School. We knew that something grand was happening in our midst each Sunday—and we wanted the world to know it. Our movable signs offered an opportunity to share this "idea" with weekend travelers, and the local highway department, on one holiday weekend, did not feel obligated to remove our signs before we did!

St. Peter's also sent out a community mailing before Christmas and Easter, and in the middle of the summer we mailed another, this one particularly aimed toward folks who had just moved to a new home. We identified them by using a U.S. Postal Service list of neighborhood addresses that had changed recently. Such a list can be purchased from the post office, and the list itself can be broken into discrete mail delivery routes. We crafted a brief letter of welcome; envelopes were then stamped, addressed, and stuffed on Sunday morning with the letter and an information packet. Other congregations report using gas, electric, and water company lists of new customer hook-ups to identify newcomers. But of all the advertising we did, the movable signs that were "put to bed" after Sunday morning by members who had "adopted" them got the best response.

Making Sunday School Lively and Satisfying

St. Peter's also paid close attention to the construction of a lively and satisfying Sunday school for children. We knew that many of our visitors came to us wanting to be responsible parents, and that an efficient and effective Sunday school that their children would want to attend was high on their list of priorities.

But here we ran into a problem. During the middle of our first summer a member of the vestry expressed concern that young families were not joining the church. They came once and did not often come again. This church leader wondered why. Because St. Peter's had practiced from the beginning an intensive ministry of Sunday morning welcome, the answer was easy to discern by simply adding an inquiry about this to our follow-up telephone call.

Telephone responses revealed that parents with children were concerned with our fledgling Sunday school. They wanted something more secure for their children. Now we at St. Peter's knew we were doing good work with just a few children, but unless we were able to communicate this to visiting parents, we were going to continue to lose them.

Because our children enjoyed Sunday school during worship before communion, giving parents an unhurried time to pray, sing, and enjoy the sermon, the few children present in our tiny Sunday school quietly entered worship at the time of the peace to rejoin their parents for communion. Out of sight, we discovered, our Sunday school was also out of mind.

What were we to do? Several years ago I discovered that consistent praise was one of the best ways to nurture a robust Sunday school morale. My two books on Christian education pay a lot of attention to what I have learned to call "show and tell" festivals, times when the produce of the classroom is shown—with brief commentary—to the congregation at Sunday's mainline worship. So we took this idea and amended it to a weekly event.

To give a better witness to our Sunday school program, we "mainstreamed" the Sunday school by instituting a student entrance processional with hymnody at the time of the peace. I also asked teachers and students to bring, each Sunday, something that could be presented as a "show and tell" after the completion of the hymn. As a result, every Sunday our congregation was shown some of the produce of the classroom (a banner made, a picture drawn, a question answered). From then on visiting parents began to stay, with such comments as "You have a wonderful Sunday school." We were in fact doing in Sunday school the same good things we had always done. Only now we were celebrating the Sunday school publicly, presenting before God's throne of grace the beauty of the classroom. "Show and tell" made all the difference.

» When Sunday school is out of sight, it is indeed out of mind. The value of a Sunday school shows best when it is publicly acknowledged with regularity.

The Extravagant Coffee Hour

Sunday is a wonderful and special time for the Christian church, a day set aside for God to welcome us, each one of us, home. As a result of this understanding, mission-minded congregations make careful and joyful plans for welcome, worship, education, and fellowship. Fellowship for St. Peter's took a particularly powerful shape as strangers and a new church met for a first time.

Our extravagant coffee hour took place in the large entrance hall right next to the school cafeteria in which we worshiped. Now by the word "extravagant" I mean that we arranged our coffee hour in such a way that, when people left the church to get to the outside door, they first had to pass near the welcome provided by a bright presentation of cookies, cakes, coffee, and juice. It was difficult to avoid the party. Our coffee hour became a special time of celebration, even worship, and it was often the deciding factor for people thinking about whether or not to come again.

An unhurried time of fellowship provides an opportunity for every church community to worship afresh in another way on Sunday morning. God also uses such times to make new every congregation's common life. When and if you re-think your coffee hour ministry, or if you are planning on building a new church or parish/social hall, if at all possible make sure that the place of coffee hour and fellowship nestles close to the place of worship. You will not be disappointed by the results.

Now I also know that the vestibules attached to the front of many church buildings don't provide for the close proximity of informal fellowship to liturgical worship. Built in another age, they don't always serve contemporary needs. So you may have some difficulty with what I propose. But I can also say this: in the emerging building plans for St. Peter's-in-the-Woods, the architect has been charged with providing such a place for informal fellowship.

From Strength To Strength?

At the beginning of the leadership period under discussion, neither St. Peter's-in-the-Woods nor Cornerstone United Methodist Church were mission-minded congregations. The former was full of hope; the latter was depressed. Their openness to celebration developed and grew because of intentional leadership. But if in either of these congregations a maintenance mindset asserts itself—which inevitably it will to some degree—to that degree their common life will be compromised.

For example, St. Peter's-in-the-Woods will one day move from the Bonnie Brae Elementary School into their own house of worship. To do so they will raise a significant amount of money. And the money will come easily, because the joy of a mission mindset looks to the task as a cup full to overflowing. This is true in almost every new congregation. God is close and new congregations know it. Grace is known to be near. Every Sunday is brand new. But to the extent that a maintenance mindset asserts itself, to that same extent paying off the mortgage will no longer be a joy. It will become an obligation. A burden. One can almost write the scenario: "They're always asking for more money," or "I don't think a lot of us are giving what we ought to." Leadership will find themselves in the old and familiar position of informing their people about what they

> *ought to give*
> *should give and*
> *need to give.*

More than a few "strong" leaders will "challenge" the congregation to "fund the dream." Backbiting and quietly conflicted opinions will assert themselves. Some might say "Things are not as good as they should be, but doesn't every congregation suffer some?" What was once a joy is now mostly a stale obligation.

A mission mindset is a fragile entity. And it is primarily compromised because of an overuse of the rule of oughts and shoulds, a notion difficult for maintenance-minded leaders to comprehend. Perhaps, however, this analogy might help. Just as effective group leadership values the process of a group's life—who the group is and the needs of persons in relationship to value both the thoughts and feelings of one another—ineffective group leadership tends to value the task of getting the job done. "Getting on with business" or "the work at hand" fixes the attention of these leaders. The work of the group overshadows the life of the group, and the life of the group suffers. So it is in the church when work news overshadows good news.

How to Begin:
Four Suggestions

1. Be sure to identify and celebrate God at work in the world.

Clergy and lay leaders seldom get stale or tired of their work as long as they remember to do this; where most go wrong is by too quickly giving up good news for work news. In the same way that it is wrong to ask children to take on tasks too demanding for them, so the spirit present in the start-up of a new ministry needs to be nurtured.

Too often this is not done, and a new leader begins to focus on the work of the church. Soon their common life is filled with oughts and shoulds, and the spirit is quenched. And after a few years lay leaders are heard saying something like, "Maybe its time for new clergy leadership." And clergy might be heard saying something like, "I think I'm getting a bit stale here."

2. Celebrate your patron's day.

Many congregations are named after a saint, or perhaps a doctrine of the church that shows God's love, such as grace. Every year provides an opportunity to think afresh about who you are and what you are about. Observing tradition is important, and communities respect one another best of all when they know who they are. Families losing touch with their histories flounder, and so do congregations. If your patron's day falls at an inconvenient time of year, the months of August and September are good times to think about the possibility of a homecoming celebration.

In making your preparations, think about these questions:

—*Why were you founded?*

—*What was your originating purpose?*

—*On what date were you founded?*

—*What was the special shape of your ministry in the beginning?*

—*What major themes show in your ministry over the years?*

—*Where does your past encourage you to focus in the future?*

—*What is God doing in the church, your local community, and the world that excites your congregation's current interest?*

—*Who was your patron, and how does her or his ministry shed light on the ministry you celebrate in today's world?*

Christians are a people with a story, and every congregation's life is a vivid witness to God's love at work in the world.

3. Value your outreach.

A new rector once asked the vestry, "If this congregation disappeared from this community, what would the community miss or remember about you?" "Nothing!" was the answer. "We don't do much to be remembered by." Closer examination revealed much more, however. Their parish hall was used every day and on many evenings by community groups, and every member of the congregation was active in any one of a number of occupations, each one helping God keep the wheels of community moving. And in their individual efforts, the large majority of the congregation took part in many facets of community life.

Catalog the gifts your congregation makes to the community, and lift them up for celebration with the bulletin, newsletter, and Sunday morning announcements. You might say something like, "It is a joy to report to you this morning that the Old Friends Day Care Community, meeting every other day in our parish hall, shared stories and pictures of their parents with one another this week. God is doing a wonderful work in that place, and you are to be thanked for helping God make that possible."

Praise and thanksgiving go a long way in the growth of self-esteem. Congregations who are reminded too often about what they are not doing and what they need to be doing suffer from low-grade self-esteem and depression that makes singing any song difficult.

4. Value resistance to newness.

Whenever newness shows in any family or organization, resistance also takes shape. It is to be expected. And often resistance comes from the most unlikely sources. A personal story illustrates this: several years ago the grandmother of my children brought a new and more creative version of the traditional candied yams to our Thanksgiving Day table. Our teenaged daughters were extremely miffed; one would have thought the end of the world had arrived. Their "Nanny" had spoiled a dish they were growing to love.

Resistance is the way human beings adapt to and accept change. It provides a bridge between the old and the new, and it demands to be valued as legitimate; otherwise, resistance will harden and destroy any possibility of further conversation.

Should you try some of the ideas presented in this book, from some quarters there will be resistance. Listen to it. Help give it voice. Be patient with it. But also remember Whose ministry the church first of all serves, and evaluate any change first of all from the perspective of how it might serve God more adequately than the present way of doing things.

Most congregations go wrong because in dealing with change

1) *they are disturbed by resistance because they don't expect it;*

2) *they are not expecting it, so they don't welcome it as an expression of movement;*

3) *they forget to be patient with it; and*

4) *in their concern with resistance they forget Whose ministry they are serving in the first place.*

At times like these, prayer is crucial.

Questions
for Discussion

1. What ideas in this chapter generate excitement for you in relation to your congregation and the leadership of it? List your ideas. Share them with others.

2. What areas of ministry are most important to your congregation at the present time? For example, is it initiating a building fund, welcoming newcomers, etc.? Brand new congregations will have one set of interests and needs, a suburban congregation another set, an older, established congregation still another. What are yours?

3. Where do you see God at work in these areas of ministry? For what purpose is God making use of them? What can your congregation do to provide more effective help to God?

Chapter 7

REMAKING THE VISION

Rethinking Your Church's Mission

Highlights By now you may be wanting to take action on some of the ideas presented in the preceding chapters. Many congregations are tired of merely surviving. This chapter is written to help you think through the task of moving a congregation from maintenance to mission and to learn how to revise your church's mission statement.

Starting the Conversation
in Your Congregation

Before looking at the ways and means to move any congregation from maintenance to mission, this fact must be noted: some congregations are perfectly happy where they are. If your congregation is somewhat intractable in its affection for a maintenance mindset, and if they simply can't get excited about the ministry of identifying and celebrating God at work in the world, it might be necessary for you to put their orientation to critical scrutiny, showing where it is found and why it does not work. But this approach, when overused, sounds like the nagging it basically is. When a maintenance mindset is well established, it might be too much to hope for redemption, as the following stories attest.

The newly called minister began, on the basis of his "call" and their hopes, to open the church's official board meetings with prayer and brief Bible study. That was all right for awhile, but members began to resent the fact that more important business matters were being postponed. Upset that meetings were now thirty minutes longer than previously, in less than a year they asked for their pastor's resignation.

Now you might suppose that he was too autocratic in moving them in this direction, perhaps imposing his agenda on the board, or he prayed poorly, or he led an inadequate Bible study, but that was not the case. In fact, this board thought its task was to provide the oversight of the business affairs of the congregation—nothing more and nothing less. Their pastor's vision of ministry turned out not to be their vision, although when he was called the congregation said they were looking for someone to lead them in more spiritual directions.

Another minister requested that his vestry devote the beginning of every vestry meeting to a brief discussion of some of the points made in Church Growth and the Power of Evangelism. *One new member threatened to resign if the vestry was going to devote itself to "reading books" or studying "evangelism." Later he did resign when the rector asked the members of the vestry to rotate the responsibility for opening prayer. "That's why we hired you," he said on his way out the door.*

On the other hand, still another minister wrote me to say that because of his interest in *Church Growth,* his vestry decided to begin a brief exploration of selected portions at the beginning of every meeting. A year later he wrote with joy to say that "You won't believe this, but the vestry voted the other evening to begin every meeting with a twenty-minute discussion of mission-minded Christianity."[1]

Growing a Mission-Minded Congregation

If you want to help your congregation become more explicit in its capacity to celebrate the things of God in the world, there are several ways to proceed. But it is important to keep in mind that a mission mindset cannot be coerced or forced. It cannot be adopted because it's what the church

ought to do
should do or even
needs to do.

Instead, a mission mindset is cultivated by learning to value the ministry of God at work in the world. Hence, for church leaders the task is simply this: teach and preach Bible stories of God at work in the world, and your people will learn from you to identify and celebrate God at work in the world today. To the extent that you learn to say thank you to God for the many blessings that come your way, your people will learn to say thank you for the blessings that come their way. Learn to look for signs of God's presence and ministry in everyday life, identify and celebrate them—and your people will do the same thing. Soon you will become a thankful people who see the cup of your lives running over with more blessings than you ever imagined.

The following suggestions are offered to help you develop within your congregation an ability to handle the things of God. When approached with curiosity and enthusiasm, each suggestion provides an opportunity for any congregation so inclined to move toward mission.

1. Develop a more explicit mission mindset in your church.

In small study groups, explore the concepts of mission and maintenance. Where do you see signs of a maintenance-minded attitude at work? Where do you see signs of a mission-minded attitude at work? The common life of every congregation shows signs of both attitudes, but many congregations lean more toward maintenance than mission. With a tentative diagnosis made, share it with one another.

For a more formal process for reflection, try the following *Internal Spiritual Renewal Program*.[2] It is most effective when adapted by a locally chosen planning team.

Here's how the program works. First, personally invite every member of the congregation to participate. Then:

1. *Divide everyone who accepts into groups of six to ten persons.*
2. *Covenant to meet one evening per week for six weeks. This meeting could include a meal.*
3. *Each day read a section of Scripture, previously chosen by the planning team.*
4. *Agree to pray daily for each group member.*
5. *Read a previously designated chapter in this book every week.*
6. *Expect great things to happen.*

The format of each meeting should include the following elements:

1. *Begin with a brief period of silence to center the group.*
2. *Invite shared, verbal, personal prayer.*
3. *Conclude the prayers with the Lord's Prayer.*
4. *Discuss the week's Bible study material.*
5. *Share ideas and questions from the readings suggested in this book.*
6. *Share a personal event from the week that shows God at work in the world.*
7. *Form a circle of closing prayer, and pray for each member of the group by name.*
8. *At the end of this six-week period, a seventh meeting combining all groups would close the journey.*

2. *Open all your church meetings with prayer.*

Do not simply offer a "general" prayer or one to get everyone's attention and settle down the participants. Truly pray, inviting everyone to enter in, and offer praise to God for the blessings all around and particularly in your congregation's common life. This action will help you become more explicit in your identification of the gifts God gives. The following two questions are designed to help with this task:

— *What wonderful blessings has God visited on you since we last met?*

— *What happened to you since our last meeting that you hope will never happen again?*

Both questions help group members become more intentional about the daily ministry of God in the midst of life. Question two, however, will likely raise tough questions on the order of "If God is so good then why do bad things happen?" The discussion in chapter three might help with this question.

3. *Learn to value stories of God's action in the midst of life.*

Learn to look for turning points, and use Scripture's witness to suggest interpretations. Ask yourself questions like, "Where did the blind see, the deaf hear, the lame walk?" As a result, expect to see a greater sense of joy to show as your congregation begins to see signs of God's love everywhere.

But also know this. Because God is an invisible presence in the midst of life, mission-minded congregations also know that the capacity to speak of God takes work. It does not develop overnight, and a simple language of faith must be employed.

4. *Value your congregation's daily work in the world.*

Learn to value the jobs members of the congregation hold and the daily callings to which they commit themselves. Give voice to your thoughts as you consider the ways in which you in your daily work help God take care of God's world. Moreover, in your support of community soup kitchens, housing for the homeless, forceful pursuit of righteousness in the legislature and in the board room, you and the whole congregation are a sign of God's love. The reorganization and refocusing of your congregation's ministry will not be accomplished overnight. So be patient, but also be persistent.

Rethinking Your Mission Statements

Just about every church today is encouraged by denominational executives to construct some kind of vision or mission statement. These declarations are devised to make the purpose or ministry of any congregation more intentional. But many of these statements are mostly given to maintenance, and so, instead of generating health and hope in the church, they generate quiet despair.

The old paradigm of church leadership believes that a well-crafted vision or mission statement is clear about the work of the church, which these leaders conceive of as a series of tasks to be accomplished. This list of oughts and shoulds invariably depresses the church. The new paradigm of church leadership, however, believes that every mission or vision statement must first of all celebrate God's work in the world, and only then announce the joyful opportunity God's ministry presents. This contrast in focus makes all the difference.

Maintenance-minded leaders who are concerned with helping the local church come to terms with its purpose through the use of task-oriented mission statements believe such aids will help local congregations become more intentional about their ministry. Indeed, such statements do prove helpful, at least initially. They assist the church focus more clearly on its ministry. But once they are formulated these statements are mostly forgotten, relegated to a place in the Sunday bulletin or on church letterhead. Why is this so?

I believe these statements are often dismissed because the faithful mind of the church realizes—unconsciously in many cases—that these items are not in fact representative of the mission of the church. Their dismissal is, in an obtuse way, a sign of the health of the church. Here's why.

Contemporary mission statements are not really mission statements at all. They are statements about maintenance. They say little about what God is doing in the world and much about what the church should be doing in the world. One might argue they are concerned more with strategy than mission. More, they tend to elicit in the reader thoughts like "I know we should be doing that."

Look at the following mission statement and consider this question: Is the subject of this statement the *work of God*, or is it the *work of the church*?

St. Thomas's is a community which worships, learns, and works together, striving always to know and do God's will and to share the Good News of God in Christ. We honor our Episcopal Church tradition, our diversity, and our commitment to caring, so we seek to offer wider hospitality, deeper spiritual nurture, and growing outreach in the world we are called to serve. We encourage you to journey with us.

Although God's name is mentioned, not once does this statement mention the wonderful work of God in the world creating miracles in our behalf every day. Instead it retells, every time its members read it, what they

> *need to do,*
> *ought to do,*
> *and should do.*

The subject of this statement is the ministry of the church— not God. This is not the liberating gospel: it is work news, not good news. Indeed, statements like these are words that depress the life of a congregation.

Analyze this mission statement from St. Thomas's with me further. The focus is on the church: "a community which worships, learns, and works." This church honors its "tradition, diversity, and commitment to caring." The focus of the statement is also on the church's work: striving always to know, striving always to do, striving always to share. As part of that work, they seek to offer hospitality, to offer spiritual nurture, and to reach out.

Sounds like work, doesn't it? Sounds tiring, doesn't it? Now you tell me: in a tired and broken world hungry to hear of God, does this statement sound a word of good news or work news?

No one would argue that there is work in the world for the church to do. But each time "maintenance statements" are read, rather than raising our sights higher, they stress the ways in which the congregation is likely to fall short. And no one likes to fail.

> A vision or mission statement ought not be one of evaluation and judgment of the ministry of the church, but one fundamentally celebrating the work of God in the world.

So how could the "maintenance" statement from St. Thomas's be made more expressive of a mission mindset? How could it be revised to more accurately celebrate the gospel? Revised statements would explicitly identify and celebrate God at work in the world. And such a celebration of God's action would set a context for an elaboration of the ministry of that congregation in the world. How about this?

God is at work in the world, in our community, and in our church, every day working miracles in our behalf, helping the blind to see, the deaf to hear, and the lame to walk. In response, St. Thomas's rejoices in worshiping, learning, and working together, each day met by God and sharing with the world the Good News of God in Christ.

Honored to present our Episcopal Church tradition to the world, along with our diversity and our commitment to caring, we are privileged to offer in God's name wide hospitality, deep spiritual nurture, and growing outreach in the world we are permitted by God to serve.

We encourage you to journey with us. You will find God in this place.

Like the original, this revised statement is not well served by its length. It needs to be more closely edited. But which would you leave out: the celebration of God at work in the world, or the work of the church in the world?

Whereas the original statement has the church as its subject, the revised statement features God at work in the world. It stresses God's action and the church's joyful response in the form of worship and service, while the original offers a ponderous description about what the church is called (by whom, one wonders) to be and do.

Still another congregation's vision statement reads as follows. What might be wrong with it?

To Make Disciples Who Make Disciples!

At first glance this vision statement counts several good marks; it is bright, breezy and to the point. Easily remembered, it reads like a slogan. But what's good for Madison Avenue may not be good for the gospel. In fact, not once does it mention the work of God in the world. Moreover, it says to the church, "Your ministry is the important work in this church, and there is work that you

> *should be about,*
> *ought to be about, and*
> *need to be about.*

This catchy statement also tends to objectify the world, as if the world were an "object" to be converted. In fact it is the reverse and an important gospel point is missed: *when the ministry of God at work in the world is celebrated, conversion will occur and disciples will be made.* In the 1930s Martin Buber published a small book that wonderfully challenged the church. Called simply *I and Thou,* Buber distinguished between "I" and "Thou" relationships, and "I" and "It" relationships. A statement like this one tends to treat humans in the world as objects—as "its"—not as subjects—"thou's"—for whom Christ gave his life.

What kind of engine will a brief mission statement like this fuel in the local church? It is likely to be a work engine, not the celebrative engine of a mission mindset. Still, some might say that for the sake of being memorable, brevity must override all other considerations. With this thought in mind, perhaps we should have the *Readers' Digest* condense the Bible to a few chapters for ease of use!

So how might this brief statement be amended with good news perspectives? It will be longer, but it is also more likely to be remembered with joy. How about this?

> *God is everyday at work in the world,*
> *doing in our midst infinitely more than*
> *we can ask or imagine.*
> *Having been discipled by God,*
> *we count it a blessing to participate*
> *in his ministry of making a broken world whole.*

Wordier? Certainly! More heaven-centered than earth-centered? For sure! More good news than work news? I believe so. Will it fly? That's your decision.

In fact, most so-called mission statements are forgettable because they don't lift the sights of Christians to heavenly things. Good news is what the church and the world longs to hear, good news about God at work in the world and in our lives.

Another contemporary mission statement follows, and below it is a possible mission-minded revision. Notice the shift in subject, voice, and vision.

The mission of St. Francis's Church is to be a community of faith, open to the presence of God among us. It is our conviction that if such openness is genuine, all the good activities of the church will flow from it. We expect, among other things, to enjoy the joyful worship of....

God at work in the world, doing a wonderful work in the world and in this church, elicits from the Church of St. Francis a song of thanksgiving. In thankful response, everyday expecting miracles from God's hand, this congregation declares with joy that we are a community of faith who enjoy the joyful worship of....

The subject in the original statement is the church and the church's ministry. There is not one active verb describing God's glorious ministry in our midst. The statement itself is full of implicit oughts and shoulds. One gets tired reading it. And still some wonder why the enthusiasm of the church has fled. The revision, on the other hand, is more likely to generate joy, hope, and confidence. God is with us, claims the Bible, and the church has been sustained by this truth since before the first century. Why then doesn't the church celebrate this truth more frankly and fully?

One final vision statement offers the opportunity to think more fully about celebrating the gospel in the world:

*The mission of St. Swithin's is
to restore all people to unity
with God and each other
in Christ.*

Although nicely simple, it is quickly apparent that the subject of this vision is the church, not God—a statement about what the church ought to be doing, not what God is doing in the world. "Well," you say, "the way it's worded is not really important. Everyone knows what it means." On the contrary, definitions are important. A statement of mission is an expression of vision.

So, while working informally with this small group of leaders, I suggested the following refocus:

> *God is at work in the world and in this church, every day generating countless blessings for the world and for all of us. We therefore commit ourselves with joy to work for the restoration of all people to unity with God and each other, in Christ.*

Vision statements can actually trivialize the gospel. Instead of celebrating the work of God in the world and lifting the vision and spirit of the church to higher things, to truly good news, statements often name the responsibilities and obligations of the church, focusing the church on itself, on truly work news. Any way you look at it, the work of the church is not the good news which the church or the world longs to hear.

Seven Steps for Revising
Your Mission Statement

The following exercise in revising mission statements lends itself to a leader's retreat, or a series of conversations spread over several months as part of a board, session, or vestry deliberations. Don't think you have to begin afresh with a clean sheet of paper. Work to capture the difference between a "mission" statement and a "maintenance" statement.

1. *Examine the subject in your mission statement.* Read through the statement carefully. Who is the subject who acts? Is it God or is it the church? Is your statement stronger on theology or ecclesiology? What distinguishes the two?

2. *Examine the voice in your mission statement.* Is it written in the passive voice or is it written in the active voice? Does it present God as a Subject who acts? One can generally say that an active voice lifts the sights of the reader to higher or heavenly things, while a passive voice offers a ponderous description about what the church is called, even obligated, to be or to do.

3. *Consider God's action in the world, and think about God's action in relation to your mission statement.* What can you say about the wonderful work of God in the world? To develop a snap-shot, even generic description of God's ministry in your church and in the world, consider God's newness-making ministry as Jesus reveals it, at work in the world helping the blind see, the deaf hear, and the lame walk.

4. *Consider God's action in your church and community.* Use the following questions to help you identify God at work in your church, your local community, and the world.

a. Where do you see signs of God working in your *church* and in your *community,* helping the blind to see, the deaf to hear, the lame to walk, and providing the poor in spirit a word of good news? Remember to be careful in distinguishing between *God at work* and the *church at work.*

b. How is God mobilizing your church and/or the local community to take action in behalf of those who need help?

5. *Rewrite your statement.* By this time you will probably have several notes and ideas in hand. If you have not already, write a first draft and remember it *is* a draft. Your writing will probably take several revisions before you are satisfied that you have faithfully represented God's ministry and its relationship to the ministry of your church.

6. *Edit your new statement.* Mission and vision statements are best kept brief, so edit it closely—but don't leave out the gospel.

7. *Share and evaluate.* Share your vision with the congregation, ask for their consultation and celebration, and refine as and if necessary.

Questions
for Discussion

With the basic diagnostic tools and perspectives from this chapter in hand, test your ability to distinguish a mission from a maintenance mindset by evaluating the following congregational mission statements.

"I believe that the heart of ministry is service to others in need."

"The Christian church exists to offer help to the suffering and the needy, no matter their race, color or creed."

"A congregation's only reason for existence is for people to carry out ministry in the world and to help them learn to live out meaningful lives. Congregations are in the business of equipping people for ministry."

Do you see too much of an emphasis on "our" ministry in the world, and little or no emphasis on the ministry of God at work in the world?

Chapter 8

HOPE FOR THE FUTURE

Forming a New Paradigm for Church Leadership

What does inspired leadership look like? Drawing on the principles put forth in this book, this final chapter presents a new paradigm and sketches the work of inspired leadership in three areas that are often stumbling blocks for church leaders: evangelism, preaching, and stewardship.

The Power of Paradigms

More and more clergy and lay leaders are redrawing their picture of what constitutes effective leadership. They are shifting their paradigms and models of leadership from survival to celebration, from maintenance to mission. A leader who is focused on mission, however, believes that when the first work (not works) of the church is that of celebrating God at work in the world, then all else falls into place. Hence, these leaders are intentional about always putting *God* first, not the works of the church, a distinction with which a maintenance mindset has trouble.

Earlier I cited Joel Barker's video, "Discovering the Future: The Business of Paradigms," which gives several examples of the way in which paradigms can blind us to the way things are. As Barker presents it, a paradigm is useful when it tells us what is important and what is not. For example: "Don't talk to strangers," "Brush your teeth after every meal," "Don't drive while drinking," "Keep off the grass." Paradigms are useful guides. All of us have these useful guides.

But as helpful as they are, paradigms also blind us to other ways of doing things. Barker gives two illustrations of the ways in which our paradigms can blind us:

> In the sixteenth century Galileo was imprisoned and finally exiled because he insisted that the earth revolves around the sun. Galileo's new way of looking at things, his new paradigm, one based on careful scientific observation, did not match the paradigm already in place. People in his world thought he was wrong because they were unable to see the truth he put right before their eyes.
>
> In 1968 the Swiss watchmaking industry controlled sixty-five percent of the world's watchmaking market. Ten years later they commanded less than ten percent; fifty thousand of that country's sixty-five thousand watchmakers were out of work. Japan then "owned" the market. What happened? The Japanese had refined and developed the quartz watch movement, a technology—surprise!—first discovered by Swiss technicians themselves.
>
> "Well," you ask, "why didn't the Swiss develop their own discovery?" Here's why. The quartz watch did not fit the rules and regulations that defined a "real" watch to the Swiss—it did not have a mainspring, it did not have hands, it did not "fit" the model of what most every Swiss watchmaker "knew" constituted a real watch—so the Swiss gave it up. The successful past of the Swiss watch industry blocked their vision of the future.

A maintenance mindset is a paradigm. Its most fundamental assumption is that the work of the church is doing good works in the world. In the main this paradigm centers the ministry of the church on both *issues* and *programs:* issues like hunger, racism, and sexism, and programs to house the poor, feed the hungry, heal the sick, and educate our children, and still more programs to raise the money to support them all. There is of course an important place for issue identification and programming in the Christian church. But not as the first order of business in the church.

A mission-centered, celebrative attitude is also a paradigm. Its most fundamental assumption is that the work of the church is celebrating God, not the church, at work in the world. Let's look at the ways this paradigm of mission and celebration reveals itself in some of the essential leadership tasks of the church.

> » The business of paradigms simply says that what we believe about God makes a fundamental difference in the way we conceive and exercise ministry in the church.

Celebrating Evangelism

The old paradigm of church leadership assumes that the best way to encourage evangelism in the church is to tell the church to do it. All you need to do is provide a list of what ought to be done to accomplish this task. Many church members struggle with evangelism (and disappoint their leaders) because they are apprehensive, even resistant about this ministry. Why? Because many of us have been taught, as we grew to maturity in the church, that evangelism means telling others what they

> *ought to believe*
> *(just as we have been taught), and not*
> *what God is doing in the world.*

Telling the world what it needs to believe is maintenance-minded Christianity, plain and simple.

When confronted with the possibility of evangelism and assuming that evangelism means changing a person's belief structure, many Christians simply resist selling their friends and neighbors on their own world view, no matter how valuable it may be to them.

The new paradigm of church leadership, on the other hand, takes a different tack toward evangelism. Knowing that the more the church is able to see God at work every day in the world, and knowing also that Scripture, when used to show God at work in the world through the ministry of preaching and teaching, is a resource without comparison, these leaders have learned that the wonderful ministry of evangelism then takes a natural and spontaneous shape in the church.

A celebrating church gives rise to evangelism: a maintenance-minded church cannot. A maintenance mindset is often the reason why many Christians have trouble with the ministry of evangelism, while a mission-minded perspective, with its celebration of God at work in the world, naturally and easily sets Christians free to speak of God in careful and appealing ways.

> » Evangelism is *not* the work of convincing others to believe in God: it is the wonderful ministry of identifying and celebrating God at work in the world.

Evangelism is the joy of adoration, praise, and thanksgiving. It sounds more like the song of angels announcing the birth of Jesus than the closely reasoned argument of a lawyer trying to convince a judge and jury of the rightness of a client's position.

Anticipating the Decade of Evangelism, in 1973 the Episcopal Church adopted a definition of evangelism first formulated by Archbishop William Temple shortly after World War II. But instead of celebrating the work of God in the world, truly good news, Temple's definition tells the church what it should be doing and leaves out any mention of the wonderful work of God in the world:

> Evangelism is the presentation of Jesus Christ, in the power of the Holy Spirit, in such ways that persons may be led to believe in him as Savior and follow him as Lord within the fellowship of the church.

Crafted more than a half century ago, the definition itself is theologically sound and correct. But it is far better suited to the classroom than it is helpful to Christians in the workaday world who may want guidance about how best to bear witness to the gospel. Imagine what would happen if an evangelist acted on this definition. First the evangelist gets the other person's attention: "Say," she begins, "I want to tell you about the Lord Jesus Christ." Then she proceeds to lecture her plumbing partner as she sweats the joint of a supply line to the new gas-fired furnace now being installed in the basement of a homeowner.

For evangelism in the marketplace, something more practical and focused is needed. For most of us, the possibilities for evangelism occur on the job site or at the mall, even perhaps with a neighbor while repairing the lawnmower or planting a new bush at the corner of the house.

There are three important things wrong with this definition. First, although it names both Jesus and the Holy Spirit, it ignores the wonderful work of God in the world and centers instead on the *work of the church*. It promotes a maintenance mindset, telling people what they ought to do.

Second, it is a *creedal definition* of the saving work of Jesus Christ. Creedal affirmations are intellectual and theological statements of Christianity, appropriate as a short-hand expression of faith for believers gathered at times of worship or discussion, but a far cry from the sharing of stories about God at work in the world.

Think for just a moment about the shape of Scripture itself: it is full of wonderful stories about God at work in the world. When theological statements occur, they are almost always within the context of a story. "Leading" someone to affirm a creedal affirmation is more like brainwashing than it is akin to evangelism. Mission-minded Christians are much easier with the wonderful ministry of evangelism precisely because they have learned to sing like angels the everyday song of God's love.

Third, the definition itself is focused on *telling* the world what the church believes, not on identifying and *celebrating* God at work in the world. There is a big difference between telling and celebrating. Telling has an agenda in mind: it expects the other to hear, and structures its presentation with this end in mind. It is subtly coercive, and whenever coercion occurs, however subtly, the object of coercion feels threatened while the coercer, no matter how good the intentions, feels guilty. That is precisely what happens in what many today propose as evangelism. Celebration, on the other hand, is not likely to be coercive. It falls into the realm of adoration and thanksgiving, and trusts the Holy Spirit to convict of the truth.

What would a mission-minded definition of evangelism look like? Using the same definition developed by Temple, a mission-minded Christian might reframe the idea this way:

> Since God is every day at work in the world, evangelism above all else enjoys the work of introducing God to God's world, and does so whenever the blind see, the deaf hear, and the lame walk. So look for these times and events, give quiet thanks and praise to God and, if seemly, offer your thoughts to others.

A definition like this, celebrating God at work in the world, is indeed good news. It gives expression to the mission-minded christology briefly developed in chapter one, doing for the ministry of evangelism what Temple's definition attempted.

The New Testament word *evangel* is derived from the Greek *euangelion,* which simply means "good news" or "gospel." More, the Greek word *angelein* is the root of the word "angel." Above all else, an angel is a messenger—and so is every evangelist.

"But if an evangelist is a messenger," you say, "then what is the message we proclaim?" Simply put, the message is this: God is with us, God acts in our behalf, there is never a time when we are alone, and in the flesh Jesus shows us the shape of God's everyday presence and ministry. This basic vision empowers mission-minded congregations.

> » Evangelism is simply the ministry of introducing God-in-the-world to God's world, and it rejoices in using every-day stories and events.

Evangelism is widely and comfortably practiced in mission-minded congregations (though not necessarily by the name I give it). Better than a pulpit model or a "sales pitch," the words "conversation," "introduction," and "interpretation" best describe the ways and means of workplace evangelism today.

Preaching the Power of God

The vitality of mission-minded congregations is nurtured by preaching. The old paradigm of church leadership might say that strong and effective preaching "challenges" the people of God to faithfulness, to carry out the tasks of ministry with which the church has been entrusted. This style of preaching tends to be work-centered, no matter how subtle the guise. The new paradigm of church leadership believes that preaching is first of all a wonderful opportunity to announce to the world that the kingdom of heaven is at hand.

The work of God in the world is the subject of these sermons, not the work of the church.

With the intention of "setting the church straight," maintenance-minded sermons often center on what the church should believe and what the church should do. They do not celebrate God at work in the world.

One church leader, for example, preaching on the feeding of the five thousand, "challenged" his congregation to more fully value even the smallest resources at hand. "Because the disciples did not value the loaves and the fishes," he said, "they were not prepared to deal with opportunity when it presented itself." Coercion is subtle here; the word "challenge" is often a euphemism, giving the preacher permission to list oughts and shoulds. Though it may seem to sound a note of strong leadership, on the order of "He challenged the church to...," this kind of coercion is, in fact, an expression of what is often wrong with sermons in the church.

In his hurry to challenge the congregation, this preacher also missed a wonderful opportunity to value the small gifts that were already being used by God in that church to help bring order and peace to the world: a local soup kitchen, regular monetary contributions to the larger church missionary budget, their individual voices at the ballot box on election day, the occupations each member fills as God daily feeds the world. Indeed, God is multiplying loaves and fishes today as much as ever, and the congregation to which this preacher preached is a vivid expression of God's magnificent ministry. Kingdom-of-God preachers like nothing better than to work material in this fashion.

Early in my seminary career I was introduced to the concepts of *kerygma* and *didache* when studying the Pauline epistles with Albert Mollegen and Walter Bowie. *Kerygma*, I learned, has to do with the proclamation of God's mighty acts and, by association, with the miracles of God at work in the world today. *Didache* has to do with teaching about the human response to God's action, particularly as the Christian community gathered in the first and second centuries.

The focus of *kerygma* is God, while the focus of *didache* is us and our behavior—how we live. Most maintenance-minded preachers seem to be guided by *didache*. They are strong on telling the church what it

> *ought to do*
> *should do and*
> *needs to do.*

Christians in today's church hunger to hear of heavenly things; they want to know who God is and what difference God's love makes in their daily lives.

Kingdom-of-God Preaching

Not every mission-minded preacher works in the way I describe, but the following principles of celebratory, mission-minded sermons hold true across the board.

First, mission-minded clergy love the Bible's story of God's presence and ministry in the world, and they *emphasize stories about God.*

Second, these preachers often *begin their sermons with a brief declaration about God,* one drawn from Scripture's witness. Often a one-line declaration, it sounds a theme that reveals itself throughout the sermon, such as, "Our God is full of patience," if that is a truth made clear from the day's Scripture reading that the preacher is addressing.

Third, these preachers like to construct what I have learned to call *a "playful exegesis" of the Scripture* under discussion. They value setting and history, and make use of all the contemporary exegetical tools. But they use these tools to bring the hearer into contact with Scripture's witness to God's mighty acts, and they arrive at this place through play.

Fourth, using the Bible narrative as a stepping-off place, these preachers like also to *lift up stories of this same God at work in the world today.* This is a particularly important mark of mission-minded sermons, since these ministers know that God is One who acts in the midst of life, helping the blind see and the deaf hear, and setting the captive free. With these thoughts in mind, the sermons of these kingdom preaching preachers become lively celebrations of "miracles" happening every day in the world.

Finally, kingdom-of-God sermons *conclude with a practical note:* "So what does all this matter?" In fact, one member of the clergy reports preaching from a pulpit in West Virginia with the words "So what?" engraved on a brass plaque. In concluding with a note about what difference all this makes in the life of the hearer, the preacher is often merely stating the obvious. But in stating the obvious, their hearers frequently speak to them, even weeks later, about the helpfulness of the sermon.

>> Kingdom-preaching preachers meet the world's hunger by searching out every passage of Scripture with thoughts of God's graciousness in mind; the kingdom of heaven is at hand, and they want the world to see it, just as Thomas saw the risen Christ standing squarely in front of him.

Like John the Baptist, mission-minded preachers develop their sermons from this perspective:

The kingdom
of heaven
is
at
hand.

Kingdom-of-God perspectives appear in every Bible story. For example, the story of the Good Samaritan (Luke 10:29-37) provides a wonderful opportunity for mission-minded clergy to preach the power of God. When engaging a passage like this, these preachers could preach about the importance of the *ministry of human beings* to one another—but that is a maintenance-minded focus. Rather, kingdom-preaching preachers are more likely to identify *God* as a good Samaritan who visits with us all through Scripture (echoing the image of the cornerstone that the builders rejected) and, *in the same way, visits us today* when we need help (using a contemporary illustration or story).

The following example of how to develop a kingdom-of-God sermon uses the story of Eli and Samuel found in 1 Samuel 3.

Opening declaration about God:
Our God is one who cares for the welfare of his people. God is always working in our behalf.

There-and-then perspective:
The people of Israel wanted a leader, so God set about the task of providing one. Using careful exegesis, the kingdom-preaching preacher celebrates God's action in the past, perhaps paying careful attention to the conversational relationship which God has with everyone in the world.

Here-and-now perspective:
With a sturdy understanding of the text in hand, the preacher looks next for signs of God's conversational relationship in the world today, such as the raising up of leaders everywhere on world, national, and local levels. Stories could be told of leaders addressing some of the needs of the communities they served. The local newspaper or national news magazine would be a good resource.

"What difference does it make?" conclusion:
No matter how bad things might look, expect to see signs of God at work in the world.

Thus kingdom-preaching preachers identify and celebrate God at work in the world today, using stories from everyday life. This focus makes their sermons immediately interesting and practical.

You might think from everything I have said that kingdom-of-God sermons are full of sweetness and light. Not so. In fact, these preachers are less likely to shy away from "harsh" sermons than others. If God's displeasure is evident, kingdom-preaching preachers look behind it to see why. They know that God is always angry when we abuse the covenant God has with us. And when we abuse one another we break covenant. So whenever these preachers see God's anger, they look behind it to see how love and kindness were abused. This also means that their sermons are seldom boring. One minister told me this story:

> Preaching anew to a congregation he once served, this mission-minded preacher was met at the door when the service ended: "I didn't realize God was doing so much in the world. Now I feel much less alone."

Good news preaching offers good news about God, today!

Think with me a bit more deeply about the construction of mission-minded sermons. God's creation can be seen as a place of *problems* or a place of *promise*. Certainly it is both. But mission-minded preachers tend to look more for signs of God's creative action in the world than they look for the problems that face the world. Or, put another way, kingdom preaching is primarily celebratory. Consequently, the sermons of kingdom-preaching preachers tend toward adoration, praise, and thanksgiving. They are doxological.

Preachers who perceive the world as a place of problems construct sermons in a different fashion. This focus tends to generate a sermon strong on the law, and on what constitutes a righteousness of life. Often muscular, these sermons tell Christians what they

need to believe and need to do,
ought to believe and
ought to do.

Preached to convict their hearers of sin, these sermons tend to focus on "us." They are less likely to celebrate unabashedly God's action in the world. One adult Christian recently remarked to me that until recently she always found herself with a headache when she tried to pray. Working with a spiritual guide, she discovered there was not much praise in her prayer—in fact, there was none at all. "I had never heard a sermon praising God," she told me. "Everyone of the many I remembered focused on what I had done wrong. So I learned that prayer also meant listing for God all the things I had not done." Is there any wonder about the source of her headache?[1]

Kingdom-of-God preaching is not going to turn a congregation around all by itself, but it contributes a mighty part to that effort. Even more, this style of preaching sets human hearts on fire with the gospel of God's love, and a church stirred with fire is kindled with faith.

Celebrating Stewardship

The old paradigm of church leadership assumes that in order to raise funds in the church, a well-constructed Every Member Canvass should be offered once a year, the congregation should have a clear picture of what they are giving for, and Christians must know they are expected by God to give ten percent of their income. The new paradigm of church leadership knows that a modest amount of truth resides in this view, but that the quality of life created by lively, enthusiastic worship makes the major difference in budgeting the ministry of the church. Indeed, mission-minded Christians know that worship has everything to do with giving.[2]

The relationship between worship and stewardship is not at all clear to maintenance-minded leaders: "The way we worship has something to do with how much we give? What do you mean?"

Perhaps the most vexing issue for such congregations and their leaders is the annual raising of funds. It is often dreaded: "I know you're already giving all you can, but this year we need a bit more!" "I wish I didn't have to ask you this, but this year we have a problem that needs to be addressed and we need even more of your help."

These congregations go wrong on stewardship in two basic ways:

— *By not celebrating the wonderful work of God in the world, every day working miracles on the world's behalf, they do not enable God to create a grateful people.*

— *Without this context for stewardship, maintenance-minded leaders are able to say little other than, "We must give money to keep this church alive."*

Mission-minded congregations are a spending people. Because they know God is at work in the world, these Christians in response love to spend themselves in God's service. Their spending attitude is almost profligate, in much the same way that a loving father showered love on a prodigal son who chose to return home.

This positive response to giving arises in large measure because of the quality of worship these Christians enjoy on Sunday morning. In those moments, the walls of their church seem to become almost transparent to them and they find themselves wrapped in a spirit as broad as the universe and as graceful as Calvary's cross. So in worship they give themselves to God and to one another, singing hymns that sound like this:

> What wondrous love is this,
>> Oh my soul, Oh my soul;

What wondrous love is this,
Oh my soul.

And when the time comes to fill the offering plate, they do so with gladness and grateful hearts.

Mission-minded Christians give also because they know they are members of a wonderful family. And just as in healthy families parents make all kinds of joyful sacrifices because of love, so mission-minded congregations respond with joyful giving to God in the world.

> » Every year mission-minded Christians look forward to the Every Member Canvass, knowing it provides for them an opportunity to "go on record" for God, a reality that maintenance-minded Christians simply don't understand.

Enjoying a Deficit Budget

Because mission-minded congregations love to dream and because their dreams are often bigger than their financial resources, they have also learned to value a deficit budget. Now deficit budgeting doesn't mean that these folks and their leaders are irresponsible; it simply means that they value dreams and opportunities, and they trust God.

Living with a deficit budget takes courage, but the alternative is even more depressing, a point not easily grasped by maintenance-minded leadership.

One maintenance-minded congregation recently finished its Every Member Canvass with a thirteen percent increase over the previous year. But because they had asked for a twenty-three percent increase from the congregation and didn't get it, they cut their already realistic budget by ten percent to make ends meet. To do this they cut out a contingency reserve (which probably they would have not spent anyway, and contingencies still have to be funded in emergencies), and they reduced the funds available for buildings and grounds. As a result, this church of God's people began their year with feelings of failure, even though pledged income for the new year increased by a healthy margin.

There was for them a better alternative. Leadership could have funded a deficit budget, thanked God for what they had been given, committed themselves to oversee carefully the pay-outs during the year, and continued to pray and expect God to stir those in the church who had the resources to contribute more.

Deficit budgets do contain an element of risk. Funds are not readily at hand. But God is at hand, and just as Jesus reached out to Peter when he stepped from the boat to walk on a raging sea, mission-minded congregations know that God reaches out to them when their budgets reflect their spirit-inspired dreams.

The church of God is not a business selling a product for profit, so business rules do not apply across-the-board. In fact, the church of God is a product of love and, like a well of water, it is a community full of God generated fiscal resources a lot deeper than any carefully constructed budget.

Questions
for Discussion

Evangelism

1. What is your definition of evangelism? Where did it come from? If you are uncomfortable with it, what's wrong with it? Does the concept of evangelism as the ministry of identifying and celebrating God at work in the world hold any promise for you?

2. What do you think of the possibility of simply beginning the work of evangelism by saying a silent "thank you" to God for the numerous blessings that come our way everyday? This costs nothing, but what might it mean to God? Could this kind of evangelism be considrered prayer?

Preaching

3. Who is usually the subject of the sermons that are preached in your congregation? Is it God? Is it the church? Or is it ourselves?

4. If you are a preacher, how much do your sermons state information about God, instead of bearing witness to God at work in the world? For example, do your sermons say that God is love or show a loving God at work in the world?

5. How much do the sermons in your congregation tell people what they ought to do and need to do (maintenance), as opposed to declaring to them the majestic ministry of God at work in the world (mission)?

Stewardship

6. What do you think of the idea of a deficit budget and the theology underlying it? Could you enjoy such a budget in your congregation? What difference would it make, positively and negatively? What benefits would it provide?

7. How does your present budgeting procedure generate a spirit of enthusiasm in your common life? How does it generate vision? Are you being well served by your present system? Why or why not?

8. What do you make of the relationship between spirited worship and profligate giving? What is the quality of worship in your congregation? Is it full of joy and enthusiasm, or is it too tight, or closed, or uninspired?

NOTES

Notes to the Introduction

1. The idea of a mission mindset as an engine was first posed by Joy Winter, a mission-minded Christian in San Dimas, California. Joy and her husband, Frank C. Winter, M.D., are the founders of Christian Eye Ministry, an agency dedicated to bringing healing and hope to the blind.

Notes to Chapter 1

1. *Yearbook of American and Canadian Churches* (1990), 262-263.

2. U.S. Bureau of the Census, *Current Population Reports* (1990), series P-25, Nos. 311, 1045, 1083.

3. The videotape by Joel Barker, "Discovering the Future: The Business of Paradigms," can be obtained from Charthouse Learning Corporation, 221 River Ridge Circle, Burnsville, MN 55337. A study guide is also available.

4. *The Colorado Episcopalian*, "Reflections" (October/November 1993), 2.

5. Ed Briggs, "Clinton Raises Hopes of Ministry Leaders," *Richmond Times Dispatch* (January 23, 1993).

6. *Synthesis: A Weekly Resource for Preaching and Worship in the Episcopal Tradition* (February 6, 1994), 4.

Notes to Chapter 2

1. This story was called to my attention by the Rev. James Alcorn, Chief of Chaplains, St. Luke's Episcopal Hospital, Houston, Texas.

2. Steven Arterburn and Jack Felton, *Toxic Faith* (Nashville: Oliver-Nelson Books, 1991), 31.

3. Quoted in Marilyn Elias, "Strict Religious Faith Lifts Mind As Well As Spirit," *USA Today* (August 2, 1993), Section D.

Notes to Chapter 3

1. John Knox, *Exposition,* The Interpreter's Bible, Vol. 8 (New York: Abingdon Press, 1952), 199.

2. This story is taken from the "Cathedral Notes" of Christ Church Cathedral in Louisville, Kentucky, Volume 5:11 (November 1993).

3. Tony Horwitz, "The Working Poor: Minimum Wage Jobs Give Many Americans Only a Miserable Life," *The Wall Street Journal* (November 12, 1993), 1.

4. Dietrich Bonhoeffer, *Letters and Papers from Prison,* ed. Eberhard Bethge (London: SCM Press, 1967), 196. See also Thomas C. Oden, *Pastoral Theology: Essentials in Ministry* (San Francisco: Harper & Row, 1983), 223-248. Oden provides a brief and thoughtful discussion of the relationship between God's power, God's powerlessness—or self-limitation—and human freedom, written from the perspectives of pastoral care.

Notes to Chapter 4

1. Contributed by the Rev. Nancy Page, a mission-minded priest in the Episcopal Church.

2. For a more detailed discussion of the power of blasphemy in the life of a congregation, see my *Church Growth and the Power of Evangelism,* chapter 11.

Notes to Chapter 5

1. Sari Horwitz, "Some Say Board Not Taking Care of Business," *The Washington Post* (November 20, 1993), D1.

2. Adapted from Niki Scott's "Working Woman" column of the *Richmond Times Dispatch* (October 31, 1993), G3.

Notes to Chapter 7

1. The Rev. Dale Brudvig, a mission-minded priest in a small church in Ivy, Virginia.

2. The idea for the Internal Spiritual Renewal Program first came from the Rev. Robert Hansel of the Episcopal Diocese of Indianapolis. Designed to introduce concepts from *Church Growth and the Power of Evangelism* to the whole diocese, I have adapted it here for use with this book. For more infor-

mation about the program for both large and small congregations, contact The Episcopal Diocese of Indianapolis, The Rev. Robert Hansel, Executive for Program, 1100 West 42nd, Indianapolis, Indiana 46208.

Notes to Chapter 8

1. Submitted by the Revd. Sue Scott, D.Min., a mission-minded Southern Baptist pastoral counselor in Houston, Texas.

2. See my *Church Growth and the Power of Evangelism,* chapter 9. If you are interested in revamping your worship on Sunday morning, this chapter is full of suggestions about the ways and the means.

owley Publications is a ministry of the Society of St. John the Evangelist, a religious community for men in the Episcopal Church. Emerging from the Society's tradition of prayer, theological reflection, and diversity of mission, the press is centered in the rich heritage of the Anglican Communion.

Cowley Publications seeks to provide books, audio cassettes, and other resources for the ongoing theological exploration and spiritual development of the Episcopal Church and others in the body of Christ. To this end, it is dedicated to developing a new generation of theological writers, encouraging them to produce timely, creative, and stimulating publications of excellence, and making these publications available widely, reaching both clergy and lay persons.

*Additional copies of this book
and all other Cowley titles may be ordered from:*
Cowley Publications
28 Temple Place
Boston, Massachusetts 02111
1-800-225-1534